COSTUME AND FASHION
in Colour
1550–1760

COSTUME AND FASHION

in Colour

1550–1760

Introductory text by Ruth M. Green

Devised and illustrated by Jack Cassin-Scott

BLANDFORD PRESS

Poole   Dorset

First published in 1975
Reprinted 1977
© 1975 Blandford Press Ltd.,
Link House, West Street, Poole, Dorset BH 15 1LL

ISBN 0 7137 0739 9

Colour section printed by
Colour Reproductions Ltd.

Text printed in Great Britain by
Cox & Wyman Ltd, London, Fakenham & Reading

Contents

Introduction

Looking back over a gap of centuries it is easy to see the development of fashion in broad outline and recognise what one might call its tidal changes, although contemporaries could hardly see the wood for the trees (to mix a cocktail of metaphor). They were only really conscious of immediate changes, such details as the latest embroidery pattern or length of sleeve.

To look at two centuries of costume and understand what we see we must use hindsight and look at those tidal movements. We shall begin in the high Renaissance and end in the so-called Age of Reason and Elegance.

Throughout this time fashion was initiated in courts and spread from them like ripples in a pond. Thus there was more variety among the Italian city states and small German principalities than in France, Spain or England. In the sixteenth century each had its own interpretation of the current style – to them very dissimilar, but looking to us like variations on a single theme. By the middle of the sixteenth century the increasing use of printing and engraving enabled people to learn more quickly than ever before what was being done in other countries. In the seventeenth century (partly as a spin-off from Louis XIV's internal policies) France began its long reign as the supreme arbiter of fashion. *Le Mercure Galant*, an early journal, helped in this, followed by the export of dolls dressed in the latest Paris fashions – true fashion plates began after our period ends. *The Spectator* could therefore say that 'our Ladies had all their fashions from thence [France]; which the Milliners took care to furnish them by means of a jointed Baby, that came regularly over, once a Month, habited after the Manner of the most eminent Toasts in Paris' (No. 277, 17 January 1712).

What happened to fashion outside courts and High Society? There is both a 'horizontal' and a 'vertical' answer. To be historically honest one must think in contemporary terms, and this was before modern methods of communication and mass production, not to mention modern modes of thought.

Horizontal means in the upper levels of society. Gentry returning home from court or capital to their country homes took new fashions and manners as an intangible – but very visible – part of their luggage, to be quickly copied by the dazzled stay-at-homes. Without such a boost fashions took noticeably longer to travel, with the result described by *The Spectator* that 'a Man who takes a Journey to the Country is as much surprised as one who walks in a Gallery of old Family Pictures; and finds as great a Variety of Garbs and Habits in the Persons he Converses with' (No. 129, 28 July 1711). One must always allow for a little exaggeration in Mr Spectator's gentle irony, but even so he gives a useful picture of life. Movement between foreign courts was often quicker than between town and country.

The vertical situation was not dissimilar. Left freely to their own devices servants, citizens, etc., followed fashion as far as their means allowed; that is, somewhat later in time, in less rich materials and in less extreme interpretations. (Even the very poor, who had to wear what they could get, always aimed at the same effect as the rest of society.) But they were not always left freely to their own devices. Sometimes social attitudes, or official rulings, prevented it. So when Voltaire visited England in 1728 he, like other foreign visitors before and since, was not only surprised by the casual way all classes mixed in public places but took the apprentices and servants enjoying themselves in their holiday clothes to be people of fashion (i.e. members of Society) – though a second glance must have shown that their clothes were not expensive enough. His surprise tells us something about France too.

Vertically, then, fashion slowly worked its way down through the social classes despite sumptuary laws, the effects of the time-lag helping to place the wearer's social station. It would be further modified by differing ideas of propriety, the bourgeois' standards being very different from the courtier's, for instance.

We must always remember, too, that at any time and place a variety of styles were to be seen simultaneously. Old people and those of a conservative habit of mind always dress behind the latest fashion. In our two centuries different classes had their own 'latest fashions' and this rule applies to them too. Moreover in some cases men deliberately wore outmoded styles to advertise their professions, so the world could see they were doctors, lawyers, etc. (this lingers still in academic gowns and judges' robes). Also, particularly in sixteenth and seventeenth century Europe and America, one's religion was likely to show in one's dress.

The Protestant Christian sects that were becoming so important not only saw their interpretation of religion as the truer and purer, but also felt a need to demonstrate it in their daily lives. Clothes, being personal, are highly emotive and fashion seemed the height of frivolity to these worthies, a

9

waste of time and resources that could be put to better use. Plain, unornamented clothes were what they approved of; by wearing dull, dark colours they felt they looked as serious as they were. In fact fashion was alive among them too, but they were grudging about it. Indeed their dislike of the waste inherent in high Renaissance fashion is understandable, but why gaiety in dress seemed so reprehensible to the Puritan mind is a question we luckily need not answer. We need only note the facts, and be grateful that some of them described in bitter detail the fashions they loathed.

Morals play an integral part in fashion in any case. What is proper at one time may be quite indecent at another. When our period begins no respectable woman had, for centuries, shown a scrap of arm or leg when fully and formally dressed; while from that day to this no formally dressed man has done either, nor uncovered his chest. And this applies to everybody, it is not a Puritan attitude.

Women had yet another area to cover. Once married or past a 'certain age' decency had long required women to cover all their hair. In the late fifteenth and early sixteenth centuries they began to show a little of it, but all decent women still covered their heads. Gradually very modish ladies uncovered their hair – though even then they often wore ornaments or scraps of lace, symbolically, as it were – but the others continued to cover their heads, indoors and out. This nearly universal wearing of caps, and their moral importance, should be kept in mind. To keep referring to it would be a bore, but it must not be forgotten since it was not until late in the nineteenth century that the wearing of caps quite died out. However, there was great variety in cap shapes and styles; readers of Mrs Gaskell's *Cranford* will remember their importance in that feminine stronghold. Even modish ladies wore them on occasion.

Nearly universal too, throughout our period, was the wearing of a sword by every man with a claim to gentility. They knew how to use it, and needed to, for there was no police force then but one had to defend oneself. Those too poor used stout sticks instead.

Another thing to remember when picturing these costumes is that chemical dyes were non-existent, since they were not invented until the second half of the nineteenth century. Before that colours might be bright and cheerful, but were less harsh and garish than many we are accustomed to.

Something that constantly recurs in the margin of the history of costume is the occasional similarity of male and female dress – above the waist, at least. At any date, it seems, some styles lend themselves to wear by either sex, more especially if designed for some activity most often performed by men. There is a popular fallacy that in these cases men's styles must be more suitable and convenient. This sharing of styles, socially acceptable in the 1970s, was liable to raise an eyebrow in earlier days and expostulations on the subject seem always to have made popular reading.

Thus in 1587 William Harrison, complaining about outrageous fashions, asks what he can say about the women he sees in '. . . doublets with pendent codpieces on the breast, full of jags and cuts, and sleeves of sundry colours? Their galli-gaskins to bear out their bums and make their attire to fit plum round (as they term it) about them? Their farthingales, and diversely coloured nether stocks of silk, jersey and such like, whereby their bodies are rather deformed than commended? I have met with some of these trulls in London, so disguised that it hath passed my skill to discern whether they were men or women.' True, Mr Harrison seems to be writing for the edification of Puritan readers. But Mr Spectator, more pleasantly, included the same charge among the Female

Extravagances he cavilled at much later. Apparently riding most often induced ladies to dress 'in imitation of the smart Part of the opposite Sex'. Said he, 'I am informed that the Highways about this great City are still very much infested [sic] with these Female Cavaliers.' (No. 435, 19 July 1712).

Fashion ebbs and flows like the tide, in the end affecting the costume of the least fashion-conscious mortal. It does not change tidily on set dates but follows its own calendar. Let us observe the tides of fashion.

Our two centuries will then be divided into three parts:

1 1550–1620. The fashionable silhouette was hard and stiff, with heavily ornamented clothes that did not follow the shape of the body.

2 1620–70. The hardness dissolved into a simpler, flowing line, elegant, comparatively slender and more or less dependent on the wearer's own shape; this period sub-divides in two, both styles soft and easy but with different silhouettes.

3 1670–1760. A clear, elegant line, firm and definite but not rigid.

On no account should the dates of fashions be taken as precise and definite. They did not change utterly from one year to the next; even today the first trace of a style appears well before it becomes general and every popular style dies hard. Thus some ladies left off their farthingales before 1620, the date by which it was really out of fashion in London, but two decades later a country lady could still feel mighty elegant in one. However, 1620 is a generally accepted (and honest) date to mark the end of that fashion and turn of that tide.

Every fashion (even simplicity) is taken to extremes by a few. In extremes any fashion becomes ludicrous and gives rise to satire and caricatures. We are not concerned with extremes but with the main flow of fashion. In describing each costume we shall, as a rule, begin with the body and follow with arms, legs, feet, neck and head; thus building up a complete picture.

1550–1620

In 1550 we are in the high Renaissance, with its delight in the immediate physical world that included rich fabrics, beautiful ornaments and sweet scents. The style we call Shakespearian was taking shape. As we saw, different countries had their own interpretations of it. In England it seems every style was welcome; Englishmen took ideas from everywhere and were quite likely to mix them up in one outfit. This was so generally acknowledged as to be good for a laugh in a play like *The Merchant of Venice* (Act I, ii). There is more and unkinder detail in William Harrison's *Description of England* (1587), '—such is our mutability, that today there is none to the Spanish guise, tomorrow the French toys are most fine and delectable, ere long no such apparel as that which is after the high Almain fashion, by-and-bye the Turkish manner is generally best liked of, otherwise the Morisco gown, the Barbarian fleeces, the Mandilion worn to Colley-Westonward, and the short French breeches make a comely vesture that, except it were a dog in a doublet, you shall not see any so disguised as are my country-men of England. . . . In Women also, it is most to be lamented that they do now far exceed the lightness of our men . . . and such staring attire, as in time past was supposed meet for none but light housewives only, is now become a habit for chaste and sober matrons.'

The generally desired effect was broad shouldered and broad hipped, with a long narrow waist. Stiffening and padding were freely used to achieve it – from this period comes the word *bombast*, a modification of the self-explanatory bumbast (a padded roll). Through the second half of the sixteenth century the silhouette grew ever stiffer, finally seeming to exist in its own right with little reference to the human form beneath. Rich, heavy fabrics – velvet, brocade, damask – were delighted in and ornamented with embroidery, spangles and jewels.

Three items are particularly associated in the public consciousness with the costume of this period. The ruff, the farthingale and slashing.

The RUFF worn by both sexes was originally just the edge of a shirt or shift pulled close round the neck with a drawstring, thus making a frill. It developed to extremes, growing larger and more elaborate until it became a separate item of dress, though still fastened by strings – we sometimes see the hanging ends in pictures. The frills changed to deep pleats spread out and pressed into figure eights. These could be shallow or deep, flat or narrow, even in the end deliberately irregular (*à la confusion*), and varied in depth and width by inches. The archetype fitted close round the neck and tilted up at the back to give the chin freedom. Though looking uncomfortable to a modern eye it was not so, as long as the head was held up straight; but it was easy to dirty.

Ruffs were made of the finest fabrics, even gauze, and often edged with lace (sometimes of gold or silver). They had to be stiffly starched; fashionable starches imparted a tinge of colour, blue or yellow – in 1620 the Dean of Westminster was objecting to ladies and gentlemen coming to church in frivolous yellow ruffs. But starch alone could not support a ruff and this was done with an UNDERPROPPER or SUPPORTASSE, a frame of silk-covered wire pinned underneath. At the end of this period ruffs were often worn without an underpropper, drooping from the neck.

The FARTHINGALE was the first of the three historic incarnations of the hooped skirt. As it was wholly a woman's garment we will discuss it under that heading.

SLASHING was a form of ornament used by both sexes but rather more popular with men. The story runs that the Germans introduced it, and that it first appeared in the violent exuberance of a military victory. Much fun and variety could be had by slashing garments to show the lining or garment beneath; patterns of smaller cuts or pinking were used for the same purpose. Uninformed eyes might confuse PANES with slashes. Panes were bands of cloth joined at the ends so that they gaped as the wearer moved, giving a similar effect.

The most common method of fastening garments at this time was POINTS. These, rather like shoe laces in appearance, were threaded through the top of trunk hose and the doublet waist (or sleeve and armhole) to hold them together. The process was called LACING or TRUSSING. Points were purely utilitarian but that never inhibited Renaissance people, and some had richly ornamented tips. By using points it was possible for every article of dress (including sleeves) to contrast with those adjacent to it.

The Renaissance fondness for PERFUME – on gloves, beards, etc. – was not such an extravagance as we might think. According to modern ideas standards of cleanliness were low (and difficult to maintain at all) and it is easy for us to forget the range of smells then 'enjoyed' and taken for granted. Perfume was practical as well as expensive.

Both sexes wore GLOVES which, whether scented or not,

were of the gauntlet type. The gauntlets offered a fine field for ornamentation.

There were two fundamental sartorial innovations in this period. One was that people began to carry ornamental HANDKERCHIEFS. Not muckinders for actual use, but pretty things held in the hand for display. This idea that a handkerchief is an object to display as well as use has been with us ever since.

The second, basic in two senses, was the addition of HEELS to shoes. This occurred at the beginning of the seventeenth century. First the entire sole thickened, then came what we would call a wedge heel, and finally a fully-fledged heel. The famous Venetian chopine is not quite the same. That lifted the whole foot whereas a heel tilts you up on your toes. Heels added an inch or two to men's height and made women's skirts swing more excitingly, increasing the chance of a glimpse of ankle.

We should consider another aspect of the dress of the period – colour. It was usual to mix colours in one outfit, usually with two predominating – white/silver, red/black, white/gold were popular combinations. There was almost always some black, either as a dominant colour or as a foil. At one time the French court, which enjoyed extreme fashions, went in for ensembles of a single colour, a fashion which spread.

Men's clothes and women's being equally colourful, social gatherings were gay. Moreover colours could carry a meaning. For instance, russet was identified with country life; while watchet blue was so often worn by servants that it was identified with them and no gentleman wore it. Symbolic meanings, too, were attached to colours, a device made use of by designers of masques and others (so the colour and ornaments in a portrait can convey much information about the sitter).

Now let us consider the details of dress.

Men

The broad shouldered look favoured earlier in the century continued but now, as we saw, with a long narrow waist. Gentlemen wore a doublet covered by a jerkin identical in cut, into which the wearer laced sleeves or not as he pleased. If not the doublet sleeves were shown, but in neither case did they need to match the body of the garment.

DOUBLETS were distended to the desired shape by buckram or some other stiffening – this helped to prevent wrinkles too – and usually fastened down the front. The waistline was sometimes pointed and sometimes horizontal; the latter being favoured in Germany although a point gave a longer line and helped the illusion of a small waist. An artfully obtained appearance of broad shoulders and a swelling chest also helped to diminish thick waists. In the last quarter of the sixteenth century padding was used to give the effect of a (rather high) sagging paunch; the sag was elongated to a blunt point, producing the 'peascod doublet', a fashion which hardly lasted into the seventeenth century. Indeed in the seventeenth century doublets began to follow the shape of the body inside them.

The smart doublet virtually lost its skirts in the sixteenth century. They shrank to a couple of inches or less, just covering the points, and were as likely to be cut into tabs as to be straight edged.

The wrist-long SLEEVES laced on to doublet or jerkin had fashions of their own, both in variety of shape and in the full gamut of ornament lavished on them – embroidery, slashes, panes, etc. There was always a choice of styles, with one accounted the most fashionable; this, of course, kept changing. In the 1550s and 1560s it was a short, puffed sleeve over a straight undersleeve. Around 1574 came a French fashion of 'rising panes', a sleeve made of panes caught into a series of puffs. In the last quarter of the sixteenth century sleeves ballooned until they needed padding and whalebone to hold their melon shape. Later on, in the seventeenth century, the padding and distension were dropped; the big sleeves might then be slashed open down the front, with a row of buttons or clasps so they could be worn open or closed as desired.

The row of points lacing sleeves on at the shoulder was sometimes hidden by WINGS. Beginning as simple rolls of covered, stiffened buckram they developed into a curved shape springing out from the armhole. However shaped they enhanced the broad shouldered effect and looked neater than bare points.

At the wrists were small ruffles or cuffs that matched the ruff or collar at the neck.

Points also fastened a man's doublet to the TRUNK HOSE which were worn between waist and knee and came in a great variety of shapes, so there was considerable choice for each person. Every type of ornament was used on them too, it was only unlikely they would be left plain. At first they usually fitted at the hip with the padding, paning, etc., beginning at the fork; but from about 1560 the fullness began at the hips. This fullness might all come from padding, or from rolls of bombast at waist and base with just a stiff lining between. There were many shapes and lengths, all with different names; fashion favoured different shapes at different times, almost all ending above the knee. They came round, oval or squared-off at the bottom (a shape favoured in Spain); under those that ended high CANIONS were sometimes worn, a kind of loose tubular extension that ended above the knee.

There were two types of trunk hose besides the padded, stiffened kind. VENETIANS, whose peculiarity was that they came below the knee, could be either baggy or close-fitting; most usually they were full at the hips and fitted at the knee. PLUDERHOSE were most favoured in north Germany,

Scandinavia, Switzerland. These were composed of a few widely spaced panes, inside which was an immense quantity of lining without the usual stiffening; this hung out between the panes, sometimes as low as the calf, or else the fullness was caught at the hips in a puff. Benedick (*Much Ado About Nothing*) would have been wearing something like this when described as 'a German from the waist downwards, all slops'. SLOPS was a common English word for baggy trunk hose. Robert Greene describes a man whose 'well-lined purse, only barely thrust up in a round slop' tempted thieves (*The Second Part of Cony-Catching*, 1592).

(It must have been the habit of using roomy trunks and slops in this way which gave rise, about this time, to the making of built-in POCKETS for men. Before they had none, but carried a purse or pouch fastened to the girdle.)

At the end of the century there was a brief liking for straight hose open at the knee. In the seventeenth century long, full trunk hose, padded out to a melon shape, became fashionable. Their deflation coincided with the arrival of the new silhouette (see next chapter).

STOCKINGS or NETHERSTOCKS were important in an age when a well shaped leg was part of the masculine armoury of good looks. They had been tailored before, from stuff cut on the cross with an ankle gusset. During this period knitted stockings began to be worn (and an Englishman invented a knitting machine for them), which gave a better fit and greater comfort. Knitted stockings retained the ankle gusset or CLOCK, which survived in women's stockings until the end of World War II. Whether as camouflage, or to turn them to advantage, clocks were sometimes ornamented – in the early seventeenth century they were often covered with embroidery.

Stockings were held up by GARTERS – not the modern elastic kind, the invention of elastic being three hundred years in the future – but a long, narrow strip of material tied round the leg. Sometimes the stocking top was rolled over it, sometimes it was crossed behind the knee to circle the leg above and below (like Malvolio's cross-garters). It could be very fine and ornamental; in the seventeenth century the bow that fastened the garter grew very large and handsome, an ornament in its own right. Commonly, however, garters were simply functional.

SHOES developed in this period from low pumps, heel-less and often almost backless, to high heeled creations with pretty patterns pinked into their leather vamps. Fashion, of course, brought variations in heel height and shape; in toe caps (now broad, now bluntly rounded); and in the uppers. At first these came high on the instep with no fastening, being slipped on; in the 1570s they were cut out on top of the foot; and by the 1580s straps had developed, fastened with a ribbon tie. This tie became ever more elaborate until by 1613 the simple bow had turned into a large rosette or ROSE which might be made of gauze and lace and spangles, all stiffened to stand out – quite a work of art but surely not safe to wear in the rain.

Fashionable shoes were more likely to be made of fine soft leather, or cloth, or silk than to be stout and serviceable. To protect them out of doors PANTOFLES were worn over them. These were a development of the old patten (still in use) which was simply a shaped wooden platform fastened to the foot to lift it from the dirty ground. The fashionable pantofle might be tied on by two pieces of fabric, or even have a heel-less upper like a modern mule. Sometimes they were so fine (of silk or velvet) that they were worn indoors too, for show.

BOOTS, originally meant for riding or country wear, developed greatly in the seventeenth century. Pulled right up the thigh they protected the rider's leg and clothes from friction, but when not riding a man would turn the long top down in a kind of cuff. In the seventeenth century these tops widened and spread – such boots, made of fine, soft leather, were worn indoors in polite society, but that development really belongs to the next period when it reached its height.

A peculiarity of 'Shakespearian' dress is that it has no focal point, every item being equally important and clamouring for attention. Not least at the neck. We have already considered the choice in RUFFS, which developed so dramatically during this period. However, they were not the only neckwear available for a gentleman. He could wear a FALL or BAND – a simple turndown collar of plain linen or lace-edged, and almost certainly starched. It was not necessary to fasten it close up to the throat, unlike the ruff, and so it could be more comfortable. Also, in the last decades of this period, men wore a WHISK. This was a stiff, stand-up, lace-edged, fan-shaped collar, squared-off in front and framing the face. It was not unknown for an extravagant gentleman to wear two types at once, say a ruff *and* a band. True, it was ostentatious, but that was the idea.

What could a man put on his head that would not be an anticlimax above a big ruff?

At the beginning of our period, when the ruff was still small, the usual male headgear was a flat black BONNET or CAP with a rather narrow brim. Its crown grew taller but stayed soft and rather baggy, while the brim shrank. Through the 1560s the exact shape of the crown varied according to taste, for instance in England it tended to be broader and lower than in Spain. From the 1570s on, however, men were more inclined to wear HATS, and by the end of the century all smart men did so. The most expensive were beaver, with felt, cloth and leather as alternatives. Black continued to be the usual colour, except for beaver which would be left undyed. Fashion rang every change on the basic shape – crowns were high or low, domed or flat, cylindrical or conical; while brims might be broad or narrow, left flat or looped up, and grew larger in the seventeenth century. Their adornment could be expensive. Besides an ornamental band around the crown there would be a plume or jewelled ornament at one side – a gentleman owed it to himself to have a fair jewel in his hat and it was not unknown to hire one for a special occasion. At this date hats were kept on indoors and only removed in the presence of God or a social superior.

The medieval COIF had not quite vanished, however. Lawyers wore white linen coifs tied under the chin; scholars and old gentlemen wore them, even under hats (they kept the ears warm, after all), and in other cases they could be used to hide the fact that a man's ears had been cut off as a legal punishment.

Over the costume we have described came the GOWN and CLOAK, which were also worn indoors unless one was *very* informal.

At the beginning of this period the short, swinging square-collared GOWN was generally worn. By 1570 it had gone, although clerics, scholars, old-fashioned men and the middle classes still used the old medieval gown. Indeed, the contemporary NIGHTGOWN (which we would call a dressing gown) was a similar garment.

The gown as worn in the sixteenth century normally hung open in front, although it was sometimes caught at the waist by a belt. It was usually gathered on to a yoke and had hanging sleeves, or short, puffed ones when they were fashionable. There was scope for rich and/or warm linings and expensive braid – we can still see examples today in the ceremonial dress of such dignitaries as the Speaker of the House of Commons.

In the second half of the century it was displaced as a formal outer garment by a short cloak, Spanish style. Thereafter fashions in cloaks were as varied and variable as for anything else, and the man about town had a good choice. There were

Spanish, Dutch and French styles. There was a short flared cape reaching the top of the legs which might have a stiff collar, a falling collar, or none. Another type, originally designed for travelling, had a deep pointed ornamental cowl hanging down the back. Very modish from 1555–75 was a short garment with upstanding collar and dummy sleeves. In the 1570s the so-called French cloak came in; this was very long (to calf or ankle) and voluminous, being circular or semi-circular in shape. It gave its wearer great scope for draping it elegantly and, although Queen Elizabeth disliked seeing her courtiers muffled in enveloping cloaks, it was worn well into the seventeenth century particularly on the Continent. In a contrary fashion the smartest cloaks of the 1580s were too short to cover the seat.

The mania for extravagant ornament naturally extended to cloaks and their linings. In a well-known portrait Sir Walter Raleigh (famous for his cloaks among other things) wears a black cloak with white rays composed solely of pearl beads.

The BELT was a simple leather strap which followed the waistline of the doublet. It had to be strictly functional as it supported the SWORD which every gentleman wore as a matter of course. It had sliding buckles with rings to which the leather hangers that supported the sword were attached; the set of the sword could be adjusted by shifting these.

As for JEWELLERY, there could hardly be too much of it. Rings were worn on any or all fingers and the thumb. Neck chains, jewelled or not, were necessary to a self-respecting gentleman. Some had gorgeous pendants which might enclose a miniature (but these were sometimes hung round the neck on a broad ribbon). At the height of this period some men wore ear-rings – jewels, not the plain gold ring traditionally favoured by sailors. Nor could they resist covering their clothes with jewels (if they could find the money). In the last quarter of the sixteenth century even functional buttons might be jewels in their own right; one could use a great many on a doublet – up to thirty-five down the front and another dozen on each sleeve would be no exaggeration.

Amid all this splendour the only parts of the actual man left visible were his hands, face and hair.

Anyone who wears a ruff must wear his hair short and, until the last decade or so of the sixteenth century, men did so. This did not prevent a variety of styles arising; for instance, Don Juan's victory at Lepanto set off a fashion for combing short hair up in a brush, sometimes stiffened with glue (the equivalent of modern hair lacquer). Naturally curly hair, however, was encouraged to grow thick enough to show the curls. Partings were not in fashion. In the 1590s hair began to get longer, a trend that continued in the seventeenth century; occasionally a single curled lock was grown even longer than the rest, as a lovelock.

There was at least as great variety in facial hair. Men knew they could alter their appearances greatly by the style of beard and moustache, and spent much thought and care on them. Philip Stubbes commented: 'They have one manner of cut called the French cut, another the Spanish cut; one the Dutch cut, another the Italian; one the new cut, another the old; one of the bravado fashion, another of the mean fashion; one a gentleman's cut, another the common cut; one cut of the court, another of the country with infinite the like varieties, which I overpass. They [the barbers] have also other kind of cuts innumerable, and therefore when you come to be trimmed they will ask you whether you will be cut to look terrible to your enemy or amiable to your friend, grim and stern in your countenance, or pleasant and demure. . . . Then . . . it is a world to consider, how their moustachios must be preserved and laid out, from one cheek to another, almost from one ear to another, and turned up like two horns towards the forehead . . .' (*Anatomie of Abuses*, 1583).

All in all the fashionable man of this period spent a lot to dress himself in a style that looks highly artificial to us. But he had an extremely wide choice of styles within the fashion for his money.

Women

A thing rarely remembered is that women's dress of this period was very heavy. Made of large amounts of solid fabric, with stiff underpinnings and metal chains, it was not for the frail. A huge amount of material went into their huge-skirted, long-sleeved costume. When Princess Elizabeth Stuart (the Winter Queen) married the Elector Palatine in 1613 it took thirty yards of cloth of silver to make one gown for a 'bride maiden'. That was an unusually splendid dress, but in Robert Greene's *Third and Last Part of Cony-Catching* (1592), which had to be credible or the point was lost, 'A lady of the country sent up a servant . . . to provide her of a gown . . . of good price, as may appear by the outside and lace, whereto doubtless was every other thing agreeable. For the tailor had seventeen yards of the best black satin could be got for money, and so much gold lace, beside spangles, as valued thirteen pound.' In 1592 £13 was a lot of money, while seventeen yards is a lot of material at any time.

Women's clothes, like men's, grew ever more bulky, elaborate and ornamental throughout the second half of the sixteenth century. They also sported a rigid appearance of broad shoulders, long narrow waists and broad hips. The common practice of wearing a skirt open in front below a pointed stomacher, to show a rich underskirt, emphasised this, as did the farthingale itself – all hooped skirts make the waist look smaller by contrast, as well as freeing the feet.

This was the age of the FARTHINGALE, full heavy skirts held

out by hoops of cane or wire. There were three basic shapes: the original conical Spanish farthingale, the later (from the 1570s) drum-shaped French one, and a bell shape which could be more or less obtained by a big roll of bombast round the hips (which had the advantage of being less expensive). Only the French farthingale did not aim to create a smooth sweep of material. It hung from its flat top, which could be several feet wide, in fluted folds. The top itself was usually frounced; that is, it was tucked in all the way round, or made to look as though the flat top was a huge frill. The other peculiarity of this popular shape was that it rarely showed a front panel of underskirt.

Solid and stately as these skirts appeared in repose they swung about when a lady walked in them. In the first exhilaration of wearing heels, moreover, skirts were shortened a few inches so that they swung more freely and fine shoes could be seen. Big farthingales took up a lot of room anyway – in 1613 King James of Scotland and England announced that no lady in a farthingale would be allowed to watch a certain court masque because of this question of space. However no royal edict ever controlled fashion, and farthingales were high fashion for several more years.

In this period the waistline, the upper boundary of the skirt, was low; during the sixteenth century it became ever more pointed too, but tended to straighten later. At its most extreme the STOMACHER, a triangle that sometimes filled in the front of the stiff bodice, came to a sharp point well below the natural waist and so tended to curve out over the skirt. STAYS of whalebone, wood, even iron (covered and padded) helped women to keep the fashionable firm appearance and to achieve a straight, rather flat-chested look. A plain, high-necked bodice looked very like a man's doublet, 'justifying' the Puritan complaints that people's sex appeared ambiguous (above the waist) in such a dress. Fashion is no respecter of person or gender, and some women even wore a version of the peascod doublet.

Some charming jacket-bodices have survived from the sixteenth century, often of linen covered in the black embroidery that was then so popular. This sort of bodice was comfortable above a moderate farthingale, or more probably a roll of bombast; it did not compose a grand dress and would have easy, straight sleeves.

The ladies ran through as many styles of SLEEVE as the men (including the use of WINGS) and followed the same fashions. They wore sleeves that matched the dress or contrasted with it; that hung from the shoulders to show an undersleeve; or that were slashed to show the undersleeve or puffs of white lawn.

In the 1550s there was a fashion peculiar to women of wide sleeves that fitted close at the shoulder and had wide cuffs above a large, puffed-out undersleeve. This was out of fashion by 1560, replaced by a straight sleeve with a large puff at the shoulder. In the 1570s came the French fashion of rising panes, and the big sleeves that needed an infrastructure were popular in the 1590s, some narrowing in the lower part and others pulled in sharply at the wrists – in fact the only difference from male fashions after 1560 was that women were rather more likely to wear long hanging sleeves. By approximately 1610 there was less variety and simpler shapes were worn, as heavily ornamented as ever. (Personal taste decided the suitability of any ornament, of course; what was fine at a banquet was inappropriate for the hunting field.) By the 1620s sleeves were beginning to shorten – but that is a later story.

At the wrists women's sleeves, like men's, were almost invariably trimmed with cuffs or ruffles chosen to match what was worn at the neck.

There was far more variety to be seen on the female neck

than the male; which was only fair since men could indulge their fancy on their legs (i.e. varying the shape of trunk hose), an area effectively closed to women. COLLARS in the modern sense were not fashionable, but among so much choice who would miss them? Later we find references to the Italian term RABATO however, which was a sort of turned back collar. One style popular at the beginning of our period was almost an embryo collar. The neck of the dress rose stiffly and opened out without actually turning over, like a flower cup from which the head sprang. It was lined, usually to match any other linen that was visible; often that would be the shift itself, inside this open neck.

Apart from this style the necklines of dresses were either very high or very low; either fastening close to the chin or low and square. Until about 1570 the square type curved up slightly in front; afterwards it was straight until, in the seventeenth century, it rounded a little and oval necklines were also to be seen.

A low neckline did not necessarily mean a lady's skin was bared. It could be left so, of course; in Italy where the weather is warmer it was most likely uncovered, while in solemn Spain ladies usually preferred to cover themselves. The open square was often filled with a PARTLET which was originally the top of the shift but, as it became finer and more expensive, developed into a separate garment. It was fine and delicate, in contrast to the rest of the dress, and sometimes made of virtually transparent gauze. It could be plain or embroidered; cover the bosom completely or open out below the neck into an inverted V. Bare necks, however, grew more popular from the 1580s on, and in the early seventeenth century the fashionable *décolletage* was outrageously low.

Above, at the neck proper, came an outstanding feature of a lady's costume. Unlike the men she had several choices here, all in the finest fabric, often with a great deal of lace. The RUFF itself women wore in as many sizes as the men, and in more styles, although *perhaps* men were more likely to wear really huge ruffs. A small ruff above a high close bodice was neat and tidy, but the same close ruff could be worn above a low-cut dress, with or without a partlet, to very different effect. Or a ruff might be left unfastened so that it bent over and back, giving the neck and chin more air and freedom. This idea was taken further and the ruff opened out and fastened to the sides of the square neckline so it stood up behind. Made a little higher at the back it framed the face charmingly.

The same thing done with flat fabric instead of pleated formed a sort of glorified whisk, and the size could be increased. An underpropper was still needed. A variation developed, of wearing this in two lobes instead of one semicircle. Either version could be worn with a ruff or alone, so a lady might wear two or three neckpieces at once.

For these were all separate pieces. Indeed, how could they be part of those dresses when they needed washing (and starching) so often? They were pinned into place, a process called SETTING, a delicate operation; it could take up to an hour to get everything level and straight and firm.

In the seventeenth century some ladies replaced these confections with pieces of lace folded around neck and head. This looked simpler and softer, was easier to wear and less likely to be ruined by a gust of wind. It still needed to be starched and set.

In the mid-sixteenth century that loose over-garment the GOWN was frequently part of formal dress. Later, as the silhouette became more complicated, it grew less popular except as an extra garment for winter warmth. Since it could be worn above the dress or do duty for it the gown added a measure of flexibility to the wardrobe. Fitting at the shoulders and increasing in fullness to the hem, a gown was unlike a dress in that it was made in one piece and had no waist. It could be worn hanging open, fastened from neck to hem or, more usually, fastened only at the throat. Some had deep vertical slashes over the breast; with these buttoned close and the gown fastened to the waist it almost fitted like a bodice and so looked like a dress.

Gown sleeves tended to be either short and puffed or long and hanging, according to current fashion.

Women's SHOES were similar to men's although less visible. They wore PANTOFLES too (but the less wealthy stuck to the traditional PATTENS), and at the beginning of the seventeenth century they also took to wearing heels. Their shoe ROSES were smaller and less extravagant than men's because of their long skirts.

The heel was not the only fundamental innovation for women in this period. It also saw the uncovering of their HAIR. This may not have been so new in Italy, and German women at the time had quite individual styles and often wore long swinging plaits, but in such countries as France and Britain it was a big step. In the Middle Ages every woman who was married or past her youth covered her hair. The Renaissance brought new attitudes, first in Italy then spreading through Europe. By 1550 an English lady would still cover her head with a cap, over which fashion placed a French hood trimmed round the front with a richly ornamented band, a billiment, while a fall of black velvet covered the back of her head. But the whole thing had slipped back to show the front hair with its central parting.

Court fashion soon went further. Head coverings became little light caps, often largely made of lace. They were small and close fitting with the front edge (following the hair style beneath) wired into a flattened arch, or a heart-shape of twin semi-circles dipping in a centre point. By the end of the century this edge had been enlarged to frame the face.

HATS were much worn too by then, both by themselves and on top of a cap, and were particularly popular with women in the middle station of life. The Dutchman Van Meteren commented that Englishwomen were 'fair, well-dressed and modest, as they go about the street without any covering either of huke or mantle, hood, veil or the like. Married women only wear a hat both in the street and in the house; those unmarried go without a hat.' (*Nederlandtsche Historie*, 1575). By implication this tells us something about Continental women too. (A huke was a big wrap coming from over the head to cover the shoulders or whole body, often wired to stand out from the wearer.) Some of the hats were very elaborate, others rather like those men wore.

Court ladies, especially the young ones, sometimes went bare-headed, although they usually had a token piece of lace or jewel in their hair. Thus, *for the first time*, we see hair styles. At first hair was parted in the centre, combed softly back and tucked out of the way in a flat bun behind. For a time it continued to be combed, flat, off the forehead but in the 1560s began to be puffed up over the brow; soon it was dressed over a wire frame to get the desired height and breadth. The *raquette* or heart-shaped style was a popular one. Then, in the 1570s, the parting was dropped and hair dressed in a single roll right across, still sometimes dipping in the middle; the next decade saw it curled to the crown and built up higher. By the turn of the century it was frizzed and built up in an egg shape.

False hair was sometimes used to get the proper effect, as well as wire and padding. Thomas Nashe strikes the true Puritan attitude, protesting that 'their heads, with their top and top-gallant lawn baby-caps and snow-resembled silver curlings, they make a plain puppet stage of' (*Christ's Tears over Jerusalem*, 1593); while in 1613 John Chamberlain was referring unkindly to ladies' 'frizzled' hair.

For women, as men, there was no limit to the permissible number of JEWELS. They could be pinned in the hair. Round the neck might hang a plain gold chain or several heavy necklaces and ropes of pearl. Rings were worn on every finger (and thumb). With the ears uncovered ear-rings were a new possibility, while bracelets were worn even though long sleeves diminished their effect. The GIRDLE, too, could be of goldsmith's work. It followed the waistline without actually holding the dress in place, and might carry still more ornamental gear. Since women wore POCKETS slung from a waistband *under* the dress, and reached through a slit in the skirt, some articles were hung from the girdle for convenience – and show; a purse, a pomander, a mirror, a fan.

The FAN, in use in the late sixteenth century, was still used, if only for evening wear, well into the twentieth century. The first were stiff, often made of feathers, and soon superseded by the folding kind. In the seventeenth and eighteenth centuries fans became vital accessories for all well-dressed women.

Van Meteren, noting another fashion that began in the sixteenth century, commented that 'ladies of distinction have lately learnt to cover their faces with silken masks or vizards, and feathers' (*Nederlandtsche Historie*, 1575). MASKS were convenient when going to a public place, such as the theatre, where a lady might not wish to be recognised. They are particularly associated with the seventeenth century, and we shall meet them again. Strangely, they seem to have roused less Puritan dislike than COSMETICS.

The strongest reason against sixteenth century cosmetics (yet rarely adduced then) was their danger. They were made of such poisonous stuff as red and white lead, and their continued use

33

was perilous. Yet they were common enough to call forth Puritan diatribes, and references in common stage plays such as *Hamlet*. The appearance achieved would have looked crude to a modern eye – dead white and brilliant carmine making the face look doll-like. We must remember, though, that such faces would often be seen by flickering candle light, and the effect of the whole costume was frankly artificial.

National Differences

National differences in costume were very marked in this period, although most European countries shared the same basic style. In Spain, for instance, black was very popular as were high necks, big ruffs and short capes. France developed its own variations and tended to rather extreme fashions; less use was made there of partlets to fill *décolletés*, while some Frenchmen displayed a deliberate negligence. Italy, despite Spain's political influence, preferred a less exaggerated and more graceful line, was less in love with the farthingale than others and preferred the falling band to the ruff; each small state had its own distinctive look, and Venice had styles all its own. German men tended to such extremes with slashes, puffs, etc., as often to look quite untidy, and preferred short doublets; German women took longer than others to be influenced by southern fashions and did not take to the farthingale, preferring their heavy pleated gowns with a comparatively narrow line and cloaks that covered the head and reached the ground, while their furred shoulder tippets were warm in winter. The English, as we saw, tended to borrow from everyone, loving ruff and farthingale. Any European style must have seemed incredibly alien to the Red Indian Princess Pocahontas who, when she visited England, courteously dressed in the fashion of the country; one wonders what she thought of it.

1620–1670

Daily life changed in many ways in the seventeenth century. The first newspapers came into existence, so that Ben Jonson could base his play *The Staple of News* on the then original idea of a news agency. The gifts of the New World began to come into regular use – tobacco, turkeys, potatoes, non-alcoholic beverages. It became customary to start the day with a cup of chocolate, and in mid-century the first coffee house opened in London.

Attitudes to dress changed. Elegance replaced exuberance; extreme ornamentation lessened to comparative simplicity and stiffness melted into a soft flowing line for both sexes – even the design of lace changed to fit the new mood.

In this century, more than any other, politics and religion affected ordinary people's appearance. It was not only that the French influence on fashion spread, to unify Europe in one sense at least. (American settlers followed European styles, so this influence went further than Europe; yet the Iberians were slow to follow suit – it is well-known how King Charles's Portuguese bride and her ladies startled the English with their 'monstrous farthingales'.) This was also the era of great religious wars, a time when attitudes to religion mattered politically and violently. They were demonstrated in the way one lived and the clothes one wore – which unfortunately was a boon for hypocrites.

Protestants, seeing life and religion as a single whole, equated frivolity with sin. So they tended to choose plain untrimmed clothes in quiet colours, men wore their hair short and straight and women carefully covered theirs. Yet, being children of their time, they did not make their own fashion but followed the general one. Their special interpretation of it made the special effect. That visual differences were great shows in the English stereotypes of Cavalier and Roundhead. But a plain white starched collar gets dirty quicker than a lace one, so a Puritan in ostentatious simplicity possibly took more trouble over his dress than the fop he scorned.

Within this fifty years there were two main styles of dress. Neither disguised the natural shape, and neither was constricting. (This last is never true of fops' dress, and there were plenty of them, but fops will elaborate and bedizen any style into smart discomfort.) Men's clothes, however, tended to be dressier than women's, which even prim John Evelyn found 'decent and becoming' (*Tyrannus*, 1661). By the end of this half-century a third style was developing for both sexes, which was to be the basis of fashionable dress for the next hundred years. We shall look at it in our third chapter.

In the 1620s waists rose giving a long-legged look, sleeves were usually sewn in giving a smoother finish, while padding and stiffening vanished. In the first half of this period, too, hooks and eyes came into use and points died out. The second style arrived about the 1650s, providing a simpler dress for women and a choice of styles for men. Never again, however, was fashion to give so much simultaneous variety to choose from as in our last period.

Men

The waistline of the doublet rose and it developed skirts that followed the line of the waist, which stayed pointed for some years. Sometimes a row of ornamental points were set around the waist (those doing the work were hidden away inside). Ornament now frequently fulfilled a function by emphasising the line of the costume. The idea of slashing died hard. SLEEVES were either gently fitting; full and often slashed for all or part of their length; or full and soft with a single slash down the front. Open, this showed an expanse of full white shirt sleeve, but it could be closed at will. Cuffs were still usual, mostly of the fine collar-matching kind, but occasionally the sleeve itself was turned back, showing the lining.

By now fashionable TRUNK HOSE all came below the knee and looked like distended breeches. As stiffness and padding were given up a tubular BREECH appeared, open ended, loose, straight and reaching to the boot top below the knee. It lent itself to ornamenting with lace and ribbon – the design emphasising the long line elegance now demanded.

BOOTS were fashionable, indoors and out. Made of fine leather and elaborately finished, they were a development from the plain functional riding boot. In this refined fancy boot the turned down top was spread out in a shape graphically called a bucket top, which had a swaggering effect and gave an opportunity for more display. Sensible men wore BOOT STOCKINGS in riding boots, and when the boot top spread out the stocking top got big too, to cover it. Being on show now, this stocking top was likely to be made of lace.

With closed breeches SHOES and STOCKINGS were worn. The stockings still with ornamented clocks and the shoes with elaborate ROSES. When the latter went out of fashion shoes were fastened with a latchet or ribbon tied in a big bow.

Lace, still ubiquitous, appeared in greatest glory at the neck. The ruff had turned into a deep COLLAR of plain starched linen and lace, the amount of lace and depth of collar depending on one's taste and means. From mid-century it grew narrower, except at the squared-off front, where two deep rectangles remained. The new shape was called a BAND – and is still worn by some clerics. By the end of this period CRAVATS were replacing everything else for fashionable wear.

HATS balanced the fancy boots and big collars with low crowns and wide brims which could be caught up at one point (or not) as the wearer pleased. They were decorated with large plumes, and some still had jewelled hat bands. Old-fashioned men (which always includes the serious and the religious) kept to high crowned hats with stiff brims and plain bands.

HAIR styles varied greatly from 'Cavalier' to 'Roundhead'. Cavaliers' hair grew to their shoulders, waving and curling, sometimes with a fringe or a long curled lovelock. A moustache and small pointed beard went with this style, such as are to be seen in Van Dyck's pictures. Puritans, on the other hand, cropped their straight hair near the ears.

A BELT broke the long elegant line, but a gentleman must wear a sword so he was as likely to wear a shoulder belt, baldrick fashion, as to wear one round the waist. Some elegant gentlemen wore a SASH in the same manner, a style with military overtones – the soldier's tough knitted sash had many uses on the battlefield. It survived long in France as part of a *fonctionnaire's* dress.

The new styles that evolved in the 1650s were less elegant, and almost too loose for comfort!

In one the upper garment was a CASSOCK, a plain loose coat that hung from the shoulders nearly to the bottom of full breeches; it could be buttoned from neck to hem. Plain

SLEEVES reached the wrist, or were rather shorter, depending on taste. The old delicate cuffs vanished; instead the bottom of the shirt sleeve peeped out.

Almost simultaneously a different fashion appeared, for smart men. In this both body and sleeves of the doublet were shortened, showing great expanses of SHIRT. BREECHES became excessively full; some, open at the bottom, looked so like a skirt they were called petticoat breeches. It was impossible to have too much ribbon trimming with this style – rows and bunches of it were placed anywhere, on breeches, doublet, shoulder, sleeve or glove according to the wearer's fancy, achieving a fine fluttery effect.

With both styles men wore CANONS, which looked like the old boot-stocking top dropping from the knee, but worn without the boot. SHOES were most usually black, cut high, first pointed and then square toed, and with wide ribbon ties (often stiffened with gum so as not to droop) which began to be replaced by BUCKLES after 1660.

The high neckline was the same for both styles.

John Evelyn gives his contemporary view of fashion in his *Tyrannus* or *The Mode* (1661): '. . . a fine silken thing I spied walking th'other day, . . . that had as much ribbon on him as would have plundered six shops . . . the Motion was Wonderfull to behold, and the well chosen Colours were Red, Orange and Blew . . . I would choose the loose Riding Coat which is now the *Mode* . . . or some fashion not so pinching as to need a shooing-horn with the Dons, nor so exorbitant as the *Pantaloons* . . . if at any time I fancy'd them wider, or more open at the knees for the Summer, it should be with a mediocrity, and not to set in plaits as if . . . the gatherings of my *Grannam's* loose Gown; I would neither have my Dublet, or my Skirts, so short as if I were one of *Sir John Mandevil's* Dobys . . . nor again so long as to act *Francatripe* in the Farce; . . . I would neither have my band so Voluminous as a *Froken's Night-raile*, nor yet so strait and scanty as a Negro's collar. . .'

This seventeenth century fashion was unique in giving men the chance to alter their dress to match the temperature – cool open breeches or warmer closed ones. They had a wide choice of fabric, too, and dressed in light silks like bombazine as freely as in woollen cloth.

In 1666 King Charles II introduced a 'Persian' style of vest and breeches with a sash; the vest being a high-necked, plain, straight coat reaching the bottom of the breeches. The idea of a new fashion set by the English court roused self-protective laughter in France, but by 1670 a new fashion of coat, waistcoat and breeches was coming in which was not unlike it. We will consider it in the next chapter.

A sugarloaf HAT went with both the later styles, and CLOAKS were still important. Samuel Pepys when describing a new suit always includes the cloak, for its carefully chosen lining gave a finish to the ensemble. In 1664, for instance, he had a 'fine, coloured cloth suit, with my cloak lined with plush.' One wonders what happened to it in the rain, for there were no rainproof fabrics. The only waterproof clothes were of leather, otherwise one trusted to the absorptive quality of a thick close-woven cloak.

Men wore far less JEWELLERY than before, depending for their finery rather on ribbon and lace (gold and silver lace were not unknown). They did use MUFFS, however, hanging them round neck or waist. And they sometimes decorated their faces with PATCHES, which we think of as a female accessory; they were useful for covering spots or cold-sores.

In this period the formal wearing of acknowledged WIGS came into fashion and lasted, in various shapes, for more than a century. Like so many fashions it spread from the French court where King Louis (like King Charles of England) had a fashionably good head of hair. Courtiers copied them and were copied in turn; in due course the Kings wanted to hide the ravages of age. So the fashion for very long, thick and curly hair turned to a fashion for wigs of this kind. Wigs also eased the problem of keeping hair clean and looking its best in contemporary conditions, without any of our modern aids like hot running water or hot air dryers; moreover lice – a problem in the best families – were more easily dealt with in hair cut short to go under a wig. FACIAL HAIR went out of fashion – there was enough without it.

CANES, which had been for the old and feeble, were becoming a fashionable accessory by the end of this period.

Women

Women's BODICES, like men's doublets, grew high-waisted and often sprouted a short, tabbed mini-skirt. Although farthingales had gone out of fashion the SKIRT proper was still very full and often long enough to lie on the ground, giving a long-legged look to match the men's.

Skirts were no longer open in front. Fine petticoats were still worn to be shown off but now it was done by lifting the skirt, which kept it out of the dirt too.

By the 1630s there was a terrific innovation in SLEEVES. Since antiquity respectable women had completely covered their arms; now their sleeves shortened, creeping up from wrist to elbow and baring the lower arm. They were full sleeves, cuffed or trimmed with linen or lace, and sometimes divided in two big puffs. Slashes and panes were still worn but died out slowly.

'Cavalier' and 'Roundhead' styles were most dramatic at the neck. The Cavalier lady would wear a low *décolleté*; which, however, she might choose to cover with a very deep COLLAR, even bigger than a man's and of as delicate and ornamental materials as she could afford. This collar might be closed right down or open out below the neck. The Puritan lady wore a severely plain closed collar of the same size and shape, completely covering the neckline of her dress. The line of collars and dresses was the same – a wide curve – for both persuasions, the difference lying in the ornamental lace and degree of opacity (anything from two layers of linen to one of gauze, or no collar).

RIBBON knots were nearly as popular with women as ribbon loops among the men. They appeared on bodice, collar and sleeves, at waist and neck and sometimes pinned in the hair.

HAIR styles changed drastically. Coiffures no longer rose up above the brow but lay flat across the top of the head, standing out at the sides. The commonest style was to have most of the hair dressed in a knot or bun high at the back of the head, with the rest frizzed or curled to frame the face. There would be a sort of frizz of curls across the forehead and long thick side curls or ringlets. Some ladies were not above using wire and ribbon to make the side curls stand out well; some wore a long lovelock.

Where men's dress next developed simultaneously into plain and dressy styles the ladies' dress grew simpler. Their waistline went back to its natural place and plain BODICES were worn, without a stomacher; sometimes they fastened up the front with a row of clasps or buttons. Tight constricting STAYS went out of fashion and a natural, curvaceous figure was held to be elegant; for a few years women with good figures could actually dispense with stays. SLEEVES grew simpler too. Like the men's they lost their cuffs and got much shorter than the shift sleeve beneath.

The NECKLINE remained a broad curve across the shoulders, growing more nearly horizontal. It was normally low, so that

Molière could use the *décolleté* of the respectable servant Dorine to expose the ludicrous prurience of his hypocrite Tartufe (1669). Uncollared now, it could be plain, trimmed by pulling up the edge of the shift, or have a piece of muslin or similar material folded round it to soften the line.

HAIR styles changed a little too. The fringe went out of fashion, but ladies might still have one or two side curls longer than the rest. Curls were given individual ephemeral names according to their position on neck, forehead, etc. False locks were sometimes worn, but women did not take to a complete formal wig as men did.

SHOES throughout this period followed much the same shapes as the men's, with perhaps rather higher heels. Court ladies would wear flimsy ones of silk or brocade as well as leather. STOCKINGS, rarely seen in normal circumstances, might well be coloured.

Out of doors ladies wore HATS not unlike men's. If they wore CAPS, as the great majority of women still did, the hats were put on top of them.

For protection against bad weather nothing yet replaced a good CLOAK.

This was a time when accessories became important. As sleeves shortened GLOVES changed too. They lost the old-fashioned gauntlet and became longer, lighter and finer, fitting the arm closely and reaching up to the sleeve. MUFFS were popular but smaller than those men carried. Before the end of this period a lady would hardly be seen without a FAN, but these are so closely associated with the eighteenth century that we will consider them in the next chapter.

The MASK was particularly associated with the seventeenth century when it was used by every self-respecting woman. Made of silk or velvet and hooking into place, masks came in two sizes, one covering the whole face and the other only the upper half. When a white skin was held beautiful, and parasols not yet in use, it protected the face from sunburn and weather-beating generally. It had social uses too. Not to be recognised in the street, in a shop, at the theatre, gave a freedom which must have been precious to women leading rather restricted lives. Contemporary literature is full of references to masks, from Chamberlain's letters to Restoration comedy and later memoirs. Although liable to abuse they must have been considered respectable or jealous Mr Pepys would not have bought one for his wife.

Protecting one's complexion was the more important since COSMETICS were so dangerous. Respectable women had stopped using them, but in the 1650s they returned to favour. The PATCH also began to be used, a harmless thing, a mere scrap of black silk stuck to the face. Patches came in all shapes – circles, diamonds, stars, crescents, etc. – and served to emphasise a white skin by contrast, to draw attention to a particular feature or, less glamorously, to cover a pimple. As with curls there were ephemeral names for each kind.

Women, like men, ceased to wear a riot of JEWELLERY. There was a passion for pearls, a 'choker' of matched pearls, perhaps with ear-rings and bracelets *en suite*, being considered most elegant.

1670–1760

Elegance became ever more important, elegance of behaviour as well as appearance, so that the eighteenth century has been called the Age of Elegance. Whether we should think it so if transported there is another matter.

Flowing curves gave way to a sharper silhouette as the shape of fashionable dress became firm and definite once more, though never again as heavy and rigid as it was about the year 1600. As our third cycle begins both sexes presented a roughly rectangular appearance, which was modified in the late seventeenth and early eighteenth centuries to make the triangle the basic shape. A letter in *The Spectator*, supposedly from a female reader, shows that contemporaries were conscious of this: '. . . we find you men secretly approve our Practice by imitating our Pyramidical Form. The Skirt of your fashionable Coats forms as large a circumference as our Petticoats; as these are set out with Whalebone, so are these with Wire, to encrease and sustain the Bunch of Folds that hangs down on each side; and the Hat, I perceive, is decreased in just proportion to our Head-dresses.' (No. 145, 16 August 1711).

Both men and women of fashion wore gorgeous fabrics;

damasks and brocades, embroidered silks and velvets. Unfortunately modern cleaning methods were not available and if a fabric was not washable there were really only two alternatives, scouring or turning. Scouring put a great strain on the material; turning meant literally taking a garment to pieces and turning the material round. Cotton stuffs, now becoming more easily available, naturally became popular with poorer women, servants, etc., as they were easily washable although not very warm.

The evolution of cloak into topcoat began in the eighteenth century when front-fastening garments with sleeves or arm slits and big collars became fashionable. However, well-to-do people in town did not need to worry about the weather since sedan chairs were available which could be brought indoors to collect or deposit fares. They fell into disuse when towns got too big for chairmen to be able to carry their load from one end to the other.

Despite this convenience both sexes began to be seen in their own houses *en dishabille* or 'undressed', words which meant an informal, casual dress in which one could relax (comparatively). Gradually the undress grew grander and was worn more publicly.

Technology, too, began to affect costume since we must count the watch, developed in the seventeenth century, as a personal accessory. Larger than a modern watch, it hung from the waist and was easier for a thief to steal than a purse. Being expensive it was something of a status symbol too.

Men

King Charles's 'Persian' dress may have been laughed at in France but by 1670 a not dissimilar outfit had become *de rigueur*. That suit of three pieces – coat, waistcoat and breeches

– has been the basis of men's formal dress ever since. Until after the end of our period they were free to have all three items contrasting, or matching, or to have any two match with the third as a contrast.

At first the nearly straight, collarless COAT almost reached the knee (near the bottom of rather baggy breeches) with buttons from neck to hem. These were by no means always – or all – fastened; coats were often left open at neck and breast to show off the waistcoat and fine linen below. Soon the coat skirts grew fuller and shorter. It was found necessary to slit these skirts for convenience in riding and managing a sword, and the resulting flaps could be buttoned back out of the way (the buttons remained, vestigial and useless, on men's formal coats well into the twentieth century). Soldiers, requiring freedom of movement, regularly fastened them thus out of the way, giving themselves a distinctive air.

By the 1690s pleats and stiff linings were being used to give coats the desired triangular shape, which was to develop into wide flaring skirts and a fitted body – some men were not above wearing corsets. Up to 1750 the exact degree of flare and length fluctuated with fashion and individual taste, the most nipped-in waists and stiffly flared skirts tending to be French. The front edges were straight until 1740 when they began to curve back, and by the 1750s a cutaway effect had appeared. The excessive fullness then left coat skirts, replaced by a smoother, narrower shape. Coats had so often been left open, both for convenience and to exhibit the fine garments beneath, that by 1730 they had no buttons below the waist.

The WAISTCOAT, which was at first about the same length as the coat, grew progressively shorter although it retained some skirt until well after our period. It most often contrasted with the coat above, both garments frequently being heavily ornamented. This ornament of embroidery, braid, etc., might cover the front of the waistcoat and lie along the coat's edges, its cuffs and pocket flaps. The fashionable shape and placing of POCKETS was constantly changing – vertical, horizontal, high, low, everything had its turn.

The SLEEVES of coats also underwent great changes. At the beginning of this period they were full and very short, displaying a great deal of billowing shirt sleeve. They grew longer, then very slowly narrower, so that by the end of the eighteenth century they were close-fitting and had reached the wrist. By 1760 they were quite near the wrist and not unduly full. CUFFS were at first extremely deep and fashion rang its changes on them too. The earlier, very deep ones were fastened to the sleeve with three buttons (which, like those on coat tails, remained vestigially on men's sleeves long after they lost their use). Some had open seams; deep ones with closed seams were called boot cuffs – and were incidentally useful to thieves! Over the years cuffs grew narrower; for a time in the 1740s they were much wider than their sleeves.

An unceasingly popular *un*fashionable coat was the FROCK. Originally a comfortable informal garment for English country gentlemen, who copied it from their tenants and workmen, it was a loose, unshaped coat which could be buttoned up to a high neck where there was a round turn-down collar. From about 1730 it was very generally worn as informal dress, and in due course travelled to France and other countries. In 1749 Horace Walpole wrote of some French friends, 'They try much to be English and whip into frocks without measure, and fancy they are doing the fashion.' But it was long after the end of our period that the frock coat became a formal garment.

Plain linen was worn with a frock. In formal dress, however, when an open coat and waistcoat often displayed the SHIRT bosom, plain linen was felt to be inadequate; so vertical ruffles were frequently worn, forming what we would call a jabot. The short coat sleeves, too, displayed full shirt sleeves drawn in to finish at the wrist in a frill or ruffle. When the coat sleeves lengthened this ruffle remained visible. Since fine lace ruffles were the preferred kind they were often made separately and sewn on lightly so they could be removed for washing. Ideally they would match the lace or ruffles at throat and breast.

There were great changes at the throat. The band yielded place to the NECKCLOTH and that in the 1720s to the CRAVAT and, later, to the STOCK and SOLITAIRE. The neckcloth was simply a long strip of muslin, or even lace, twisted round the neck and tied in front. In the late seventeenth century there could be a broad ribbon bow behind it. Another popular style was the Steinkirk – a simple knot or twist with the long ends pulled through a buttonhole and named after the battle where it was supposed to have originated. The stock which smart men began to wear about 1740 was made of folds of stiffened muslin or cambric fastened at the back of the neck. The solitaire, which came into fashion roughly a decade later, was a band of black ribbon tied over the stock and properly worn with a bag-wig so that it looked like an extension of the ribbon tying the black silk bag.

BREECHES were worn by all with pretensions to gentility. (Not, for instance, by the poor *sans culottes* in France; nor by ordinary sailors who, for the sake of convenience if nothing else, wore nether garments cut in traditional bell bottom style although their officers dressed like gentlemen.) The bagginess soon went out of breeches and they were cut to give no more than a comfortable ease, fastened round the waist and sitting on the hips. Braces were not used; they only came in at the very end of the century when smart pantaloons were cut high above the waist and had to be held up. Breeches covered the knee, where they were fastened with buttons or buckles. At first buttons were preferred, but from the second quarter of the eighteenth century buckles were the more popular. Garters were tied below the knee and buckled breeches then fastened over the stockings, if only for display; otherwise the stocking tops were rolled over the breeches.

STOCKINGS were knitted of wool or thread or silk. In the eighteenth century white became the most elegant colour, but by no means the only one worn. A well-shaped leg was an asset to a man throughout our period, and there are malicious tales of ill-endowed fops who padded the calves of their stockings.

BOOTS were again mere riding gear and SHOES the normal wear. By the 1690s BUCKLES were replacing ribbon ties; they ranged from the strictly utilitarian to some so costly and beautiful they could count as jewellery. The shoes themselves were heeled, with vamps and tongues still cut high. Fashion frequently altered the exact shape or height of toes and heels. In the seventeenth century French courtiers wore red heels, and so smart men and fops in other lands wore them too.

By the early eighteenth century CLOAKS were only worn in very bad weather. They were replaced by a variety of new modified garments that had in common a front fastening, sleeves or slits to accommodate the arms and usually a large, cape-like collar. There were a lot of names for them, all being some form of SURTOUT, and in the end they developed into a modern type of topcoat and what the French call a redingote. John Gay devoted a stanza of his *Trivia* (1716) to them:

> Nor should it prove thy less important care
> To chuse a proper coat for winter's wear.
> Now in thy trunk thy D'Oily habit fold,
> The silken drugget ill can face the cold;
> The frieze's spongy nap is sok'd with rain,
> And show'rs soon drench the camlet's cockled grain,
> True Witney broadcloth with its shag unshorn,

Unpierc'd is in the lasting tempest worn:
Be this the horseman's fence, for who would wear
Amid the town the spoils of Russia's bear?
Within the *Roquelaure's clasp thy hands are pent,
Hands, that stretch'd forth invading harms prevent.
Let the looped Bavaroy the fop embrace,
Or his deep cloak bespatter'd o'er with lace.
That garment† best the winter's rage defends,
Whose ample form without one plait depends;
By various names in various countries known,
Yet held in all the true Surtout alone;
Be thine of Kersey firm, tho' small the cost,
Then brave unwet the rain, unchill'd the frost.

Above these clothes men displayed clean-shaven faces and WIGS. The latter were quite blatant, making no pretence to being the wearer's natural growth. Purely objects of fashion, they changed their style almost more often than men's coats. However, they all fell into a few broad categories.

First came the great full-bottomed wigs, thick and curly, falling well below the shoulders and masking the face. In the 1690s they rose at the crown into a peak or foretop which, about 1700, was divided by a centre parting like a valley between hills. This foretop flattened by about 1710, only to rise again later on in a new version as the toupee, when partings ceased to be worn.

Active gentlemen like soldiers or travellers needed something less demanding; so the campaign wig was born and tie wigs developed. The former (worn until 1750) simply divided the mantling mass at shoulder level into three short curls. Tie wigs began as informal wear in the early eighteenth century.

* A transitional garment – a knee-length cloak shaped at the shoulders, caped and buttoned in front.

† A 'Joseph', 'wrap-rascal', etc.; i.e. a surtout.

The tail or queue was dressed in one of three ways, all tied with black ribbon: 1) simply tied back and perhaps curled; 2) plaited, with a bow top and bottom, this was the Romillies wig, popular in England; 3) the bag-wig with the queue enclosed in a black silk bag.

By the 1730s both a short (shoulder length) full-bottomed wig and the bag-wig were acceptable with formal dress. Even with tie wigs, however, the face was not completely bare. Though the crown was smooth the side hair was still frizzed or curled at the temples and around the ears. This was formalised about 1750 – at the time when the toupee was rising above the forehead – into smooth horizontal curls above the ears such as we still see on playing cards.

Bob wigs, long or short (that is, ear- or chin-length) were bushy, easy to wear, but strictly informal or for such middle-class types as inn-keepers.

A man who could afford it would, of course, have several wigs for different occasions. One who could not – or wanted to show off his fine natural growth – dressed his own hair as though it were a wig. Even wig wearers quite often combed their own hair into the wig at the front, to hide the join. A whole wardrobe of styles was available. Mr Spectator, again in the person of an alleged female correspondent, describes the possible effect of such a wardrobe: 'I had an humble Servant last Summer who the first Time he declared himself, was in a Full-Bottom Wig, but the Day after, to my no small Surprize, he accosted me in a thin Natural one. I receiv'd him, at this our second Interview, as a perfect Stranger . . . in the Park the same Evening he appeared to me in one of the Wigs that I think you call a Night-Cap, which had altered him more effectively than before. He afterwards played a Couple of Black Riding Wigs upon me, with the same success.' (No. 319, 6 March 1712).

From the turn of the century men powdered their formal wigs. Since grease and pomatum were used to hold the curls in place, cleaning wigs must have been a fearsome job as well as a specialist one. But no self-respecting gentleman would be seen out of doors without his hat and wig; he would have felt half dressed.

At the beginning of this period the fashionable HAT was relatively low crowned, broad brimmed and plumed. As wigs grew important plumes grew less so and went out of fashion, while brims were regularly cocked, that is turned up. At first they were only cocked in one place. Later on three cocks at once made a tricorne, a three cornered hat, and for most of the eighteenth century this was the only hat for a gentleman. Small fluctuations in shape – height of crown, depth of brim- therefore seemed momentous at the time. The cocking of one's hat became an art, with results immediately apparent to the knowledgeable contemporary eye. The brim was bound with braid (even gold might be used to 'lace' a hat) and sometimes an expensive button was put on it, attached to the crown with a loop. Professional men–clergy, lawyers, etc. – often wore a round hat with a round brim, uncocked.

Both wigs and hats were expensive. Wigs could be hot and heavy, even with the natural hair cut short or shaved off. Moreover, beautiful, expensive and crushable silk coats are not the best things to relax in. So gentlemen took them both off at home and relaxed in a CAP and GOWN.

The cap, or NIGHTCAP as it was called though much worn by day, was needed to protect heads used to the sweaty warmth of a wig from draughts and chills. Some looked rather like a turban, others were a deep cap with turned-up brim; all covered the whole head. The GOWN that hid the absence of coat, and perhaps waistcoat, and which was quite likely to be made of cotton, had several names: nightgown, Indian gown, banyan, etc. Of the simplest cut, it was loose and full, covering the whole person and so comfortable that some people received friends and morning callers in it. Indeed, many gentlemen had their portraits painted in their gowns, and in 1707 Beau Nash, the social despot of elegant Bath, made it the third of his Rules 'That Gentlemen of Fashion never appearing in a Morning before the Ladies in Gowns and Caps show Breeding and Respect.'

A WATCH, attached to the breeches' fob pocket, hung under the waistcoat and was the only ornament one would expect to see with cap and gown, unless a possible signet ring is counted; both being functional as well as ornamental.

That badge of a gentleman, the SWORD, now becomes difficult to categorise. As towns became safer – or if not one always went out accompanied by stout servants – men of fashion could draw a distinction between a light, ornamental dress sword and more practical weapons. (Beau Nash banned the sword in Bath.) In either case it presented a problem to wearers of the long coat of the 1670s, since it had to be attached to a BELT. A waist belt would have ruined the line of the coat so for a time shoulder belts were worn, maybe covered and softened by a SASH (which could be similarly employed round the waist). The sash was more popular in France than in England, where it retained military overtones; for both reasons some fops liked it. The later, fuller coat skirts with slits or vents allowed the sword to lie against the hip *under* the coat, and poke out at the back. This mode of wearing swords continued beyond the end of our period.

As we saw, men no longer wore much personal JEWELLERY. There was, however, considerable scope for expensive ornament – and a display of tastefulness – in their dress, besides the display of fine lace at wrist, throat and breast. Shoe and knee buckles could be goldsmith's work; so could watch case and sword hilt; and, moreover, this was the age of snuff. In the last quarter of the seventeenth century the sniffing of snuff superseded the smoking and chewing of tobacco. A SNUFFBOX was therefore a normal masculine accessory. Every imaginable type was sold, from the plainest and most utilitarian to some so rich and beautiful they survive in museums as works of art.

Another universal masculine accessory was the CANE. Long sticks had always been used by the elderly or infirm, or as convenient aids when walking in rough country. In the seventeenth century they became an elegant accessory and remained so into the twentieth century. A man of any status would no more go out without his cane than without his hat or gloves. Its ferrule and head were covered with metal, on occasion gold or silver or some other precious substance like amber. Ribbon was sometimes tied round the top, which had its uses as the loop could be slipped over the wrist or a waistcoat button. MUFFS, too, were still a normal masculine accessory.

Women

By 1670 soft easy dresses were being superseded by a firmer, more constricted style. Stiffer and longer STAYS became necessary – possibly the lower and middle classes had never given them up. Before the end of the seventeenth century they were so vital that an English workhouse would issue them to its inmates.

Wearing stays of the new shape the body appeared straighter and the waistline lower. PETTICOATS were again displayed under an open overskirt hanging in a straight long line that was carried through by the FONTANGE or COMMODE (the English name for the same thing) that ladies wore on their heads (see p. 60) from the 1680s to the second decade of the eighteenth century. Then the head was dressed smaller, the introduction of the HOOP altered the shape of the skirt, and the general effect of a woman's appearance changed from rectangular to triangular.

The long stiff BODICE was open in front and usually laced across a stomacher. This style which, with a changing neckline, continued in use throughout our period and long after, soon developed an unexpectedly large variety of methods of fastening that bodice. It might be laced across a stomacher; hooks and eyes might fasten the stomacher to it; sometimes one or more ribbon bows replaced the laces – a row of them being called an *échelle* because of the ladder-like look; sometimes the bodice was simply closed with no stomacher. Or else a cross-over bodice might be worn (though this was less usual), with no stomacher but a little frill or lace filling for modesty. Down the two straight edges of the bodice-with-stomacher eighteenth-century women often placed ornamental strips called ROBINGS. These ended at the waist until the 1750s when they lengthened and, if the skirt was an open one, reached the hem.

The late seventeenth-century SKIRT was unlike sixteenth-century open skirts, being looped up and back to show the ornamental petticoat, and hanging in folds that fell to a train behind. In due course the mass of material at the back was enlarged with padding – an early bustle. About 1710 the hooped skirt arrived, and was worn by well-dressed ladies for a good seventy years. It must have been more comfortable than the style it superseded, lighter and with the weight more evenly distributed. Hoops varied in size, of course, from person to person and time to time, but the wide skirt below a 'natural' body ensured the characteristic triangular look.

The shape of a fashionable HOOP altered as the years went by. At first it was rounded but by the 1740s a sharper angle made it more conical. Then it flattened before and behind but grew broader, so that a lady was narrow seen from the side but from the front her side hoops or PANNIERS made her very wide. (The more extreme forms of this style were a gift to contemporary satirists, yet it remained popular from the 1740s to the 1760s and was worn as formal court dress for several decades more.) In the 1750s the hem rose an inch or two, but by 1760 it touched the feet again. With a hoop one could wear either an open or a closed skirt but not a train – that belonged to court dress and mantuas (see below). If open, one could choose either a matching or contrasting petticoat; in both cases the part showing was likely to be highly ornamented with frills, flounces, embroidery, etc.

This dress of fitted boned bodice above hooped skirt – called in France the *robe à l'anglaise* – was the basic costume of the greater part of the eighteenth century. Its very stiffness ensured that lighter easier dresses would evolve for informal wear. In France, where formal dress tended to be more extreme, these loose unboned dresses were accepted sooner than in England or Germany as suitable for all but the most formal occasions.

An early, but long-lasting, example was the MANTUA which started in the 1670s as a simple loose gown with no stiffening. It had a train, as was customary then, and retained it when trains went out of fashion otherwise. Mantuas were worn loose and open at first, but later the body was fastened close to the boned underbodice or stays; it was worn thus beyond the end of our period.

Then there was the ROBE BATTANTE, a loose dress which fell from shoulder to hem in an unbroken line and could be left open or fastened to the hem; this was most popular in France. A NIGHTGOWN was another name for this type of easy unboned dress which, beginning as a garment for private relaxation, came to be made in fine materials and worn nearly everywhere. In 1759 Horace Walpole's niece Maria was married privately 'in a rich white satin night-gown'. Another of these dresses, too popular to ignore, was the SACQUE, SACK or *robe à la française* (with the bodice fitted in front only) which so many of Watteau's women wear. Here the fullness was mostly at the back, falling in an unbroken line from the shoulders where it was stitched down in pleats. It originated in France and came to England about 1720, where it took longer to be accepted for public wear; it continued to be popular until late in the century.

Throughout this period an entirely different style was also worn, though hardly in public by the fashionable; it was much used by the poorer and lower classes, indeed it could mark the wearer's social level. This was the ensemble of jacket bodice and petticoat. Its convenience – economic, physical, etc. – is self-evident. There were many names for the different versions of this bodice, which was simply like a dress cut short somewhere below the waist and above the knee; CASAQUIN, PET EN L'AIR, CARACO are some of the best known. The neatest type had a fitted bodice flaring out below the waist, its skirt length varying from a mere frill to halfway down the thigh.

SLEEVES came to the elbow during almost all this period and, being loose, showed the bottom of the shift sleeves with their frilled edging, which became as important as a man's wrist ruffles. Later these ruffles, often of lace, were made separately and sewn into the dress.

In the late seventeenth century dress sleeves followed the same course as men's and became very short, so that the arm was mainly covered by the shift. However they grew longer, and by the beginning of the eighteenth century had reached the elbow. Because sleeves then altered so little for the best part of a century small changes became important. They were always straight and rather loose, and until the 1750s were usually cuffed; then frills and flounces became the more popular trimming. Like men's cuffs, the women's grew wider than the sleeve, hanging down under the arm with the lace frills and ruffles following this line.

To keep the lower arm warm MITTENS or MUFFS might be worn.

The fashionable NECKLINE throughout this period was cut very low. At first it was an almost horizontal curve across the shoulders, softened with folds of muslin or a band of lace. Next the bodice came straight down each side of the neck to lace across the stomacher, forming the most clearly rectangular part of the costume. When the silhouette opened out in the early eighteenth century the neckline broadened too, becoming square rather than oblong. The cross-over bodice was an exception.

Three things could be done with this *décolletage*. It could be left unadorned; given a frilled edge or TUCKER, evolved from the shift's edge; or softened and filled in by a HANDKERCHIEF. This was a triangle or doubled square of cambric, muslin, gauze, etc., which could be arranged according to fancy and then either fastened at the breast, tied round the waist, or threaded through one's laces. It was frequently edged with a frill or with lace.

SHOES could be very pretty, for dress shoes were often of silk or brocade and BUCKLES were the usual form of fastening. Toes became pointed and then, in our last twenty years, got shorter and blunter. Heels also changed, at first high, thick and curved, later thinner and lower. Tongues and vamps stayed high. Sometimes a high-heeled, backless, mule-like shoe was worn.

Fine shoes required protection from dirt. Poorer people still wore old-fashioned pattens but the fashionable wore leather CLOGS. These were flat, built up to fill the space inside the high heel, and sometimes had a cloth 'upper' that matched the shoe.

At first coloured STOCKINGS were worn, but by the second quarter of the eighteenth century white was the usual colour.

The manner of dressing the head changed as much as the rest of the dress during this period. The broad, elaborately curled coiffure of the middle years of the seventeenth century grew simpler and less broad, with short curls on the forehead and perhaps one or two long ringlets. By the 1680s the distinctive head-dress of the next thirty years had developed. This was the FONTANGE, named after one of Louis XIV's favourites. One day her hat blew off and her hair fell down, so she tied it up with her garter (still just a long strip of fabric); His Majesty admired the effect and a fashion was born. From a simple bow on top of the head there developed a tall structure of lace and ribbon mounted on wire, that was actually the brim of a small cap which had two long streamers or LAPPETS hanging below the shoulders behind.

HAIR was piled high too, in a mass of frizz and small curls, a coiffure called a TOUR or TOWER. Slightly longer curls at the temples, with long ringlets, completed the effect.

When hoops came in the towers fell, and a simpler style came into fashion to balance the spreading skirts. Hair was drawn softly off the face and dressed close to the head, one or two long curls being occasionally allowed to lie on the neck; one later, softer style dressed the hair in short curls all over. It was after our period ends that women's heads began to be dressed large again.

After the demise of the fontange CAPS continued to be worn, little things trimmed with frills, lace and ribbon, and often still with lappets. There were as many styles and patterns of caps as of dresses; some covering the whole head, others tiny and perched on top. For instance there was the Mob Cap, useful for working women and the ladies' informal wear in the 1730s, with big crown, deep border and 'kissing strings'; the Round Eared Cap that curved down over the ears, with a frilled front and drawstring tight at the back; the Dormeuse, a confection of lace and ribbon which covered all but the front hair; and many others. Younger women *en grande toilette* discarded caps, often replacing them with such ornaments as jewelled pins, a bunch of ribbon loops, butterflies of tinsel and lace, feathers, etc.

Out of doors a HOOD could be worn over the fontange. Later on HATS were worn, above the caps. For summer there were wide-brimmed straw hats tied on with ribbons, and beaver hats for winter. In the mid-eighteenth century hoods were attached to capes and cloaks of different sizes to make a variety of outdoor garments (Cardinals, Riding Hoods and so on). There grew to be considerable choice of outdoor wear in addition to the cloak; besides the Pelisse which, straight and front-fastened with arm-slits, was rather like the roquelaure, there were all sorts of broad scarves and shaped shoulder-wraps with long ends (Mantlets, Pelerines, etc.) which could be left unadorned or trimmed with a myriad frills and furbelows.

With these were worn GLOVES, usually elbow length; and MUFFS which sometimes had matching TIPPETS round the neck.

With all this the eighteenth-century lady often wore an APRON. Fine white aprons had long been worn by well-dressed women of the lower classes, but now fine ladies had expensive delicate aprons of their own. There were fashions in these too: long and short, white and coloured, transparent and opaque, of gauze, lace or silk, the variations were legion.

JEWELLERY, worn in such profusion in 1570, was a more subtle affair by 1670. Until the end of our period jewels might be worn in the hair. Otherwise a single row of matched pearls with perhaps ear-rings and bracelet *en suite*, or just a cross hung at the breast, sufficed in the middle and late seventeenth century. With hooped skirts came fresh ideas. For instance a ribbon clasped round throat or arms was often felt to be more effective than jewels for a younger woman. Later on this ribbon was frilled and ruched until it bore a superficial resemblance to a ruff. Then, besides the fundamental suite of necklace, bracelets and ear-rings, large jewelled ornaments were pinned on the corsage while shoe buckles, and the watch hung from the waist, could be works of the jeweller's art. The great difference between this and the first period we looked at was that the proclamation of wealth had become more subtle, and it was now necessary to demonstrate one's taste also.

Taste sometimes suggested flowers instead of jewels for the hair and breast, particularly for a young woman. But wearing flowers has inconveniences – in November 1754 Horace Walpole wrote of 'a new fashion which my Lady Hervey has brought from Paris. It is a tin funnel covered with green ribband, and holds water, which the ladies wear to keep their bouquets fresh – I fear Lady Caroline and some others will catch frequent colds and sore throats with overturning this reservoir.'

The MASK remained a necessary accessory into the early years of the eighteenth century. Then it dropped out of use – except for masquerades and highwaymen. The FAN remained a constant necessity for every genteel woman until in the nineteenth century it was limited to evening wear. There was an art in using a fan, and some ladies wielded it with such self-conscious stylishness that they provoked the satirists. Fans could be expensive; some were amusing ephemera but others were rich works of art. All were fragile and many undoubtedly got broken in fits of anger.

PATCHES and COSMETICS continued in use, although cosmetics were still slow poison. In French society they were freely used but in some other countries, such as England, did not meet with such easy approval. There, although many were tempted into a little red on the cheeks, a full make up was mostly used by those who thought they were losing their looks – and who sometimes died of it. Which deterred nobody.

During this period the UMBRELLA and PARASOL, long known as exotic oriental artefacts and already used in Italy and France, came into use in England too. At first (about the turn of the century) it was just the umbrella, which was more popular more quickly in the provinces than the capital and used mainly by women, and lower class women at that. Jonas Hanway, notorious as the first man to carry an umbrella in London (he had travelled in Persia) was mobbed for his pains. Not until the 1780s could London men safely shelter under umbrellas. Yet in 1716 John Gay wrote:

> 'Good housewives all the winter's rage despise,
> Defended by the riding-hood's disguise;
> Or underneath th'umbrella's oily shed,
> Safe thro' the wet on clinking Pattens tread:
>
> . . . .
>
> Britain in winter only knows its aid,
> To guard from chilly show'rs the walking maid.'

(Trivia)

English ladies were using the parasol by the 1760s, however.

In Conclusion

Let us step slightly beyond our time limit for the sake of looking at fashion through contemporary eyes. *The New Bath Guide*, 1766, was so successful it went through ten editions in ten years. It took the form of versified letters from a wealthy pair of country cousins swept off their feet by the first taste of fashionable life. Here are some extracts from their letters home:

> 'FASHION . . . . . Goddess
>
> . . . .
>
> Bring, O bring thy essence pot
> Amber, musk and bergamot,
> Eau de chipre, eau de luce,
> Sans pareil and citron juice.

Nor thy band-box leave behind,
Filled with stores of ev'ry kind;

.   .   .   .

In a band-box is contain'd:
Painted lawns, and chequer'd shades,
Crape, that's worn by love-lorn maids,
Water'd tabbies, flower'd brocades;
Vi'lets, pinks, Italian posies,
Myrtles, jessamine and roses,
Aprons, caps and 'kerchiefs clean,
Straw-built hats and bonnets green,
Cutgut, gauzes, tippets, ruffs,
Fans, and hoods, and feather'd muffs,
Stomachers and paris-nets,
Ear-rings, necklaces, aigrets,
Fringes, blondes and mignonets;
Fine vermilion for the cheek,
Velvet patches a la grecque.'
                    (Letter III from Miss Jenny W-d-r.)

'I ride in a chair, with my hands in a muff,
And have bought a silk coat and embroidered the cuff;
But the weather was cold, and the coat it was thin,
So the taylor advised me to line it with skin:
But what with my *Nivernois hat can compare,
Bag-wig, and lac'd ruffles, and black solitaire?
And what can a man of true fashion denote,
Like an ell of good ribbon tied under the throat?
My buckles and box are in excellent taste,
The one is of paper, the other of paste.'
                    (Letter X from Mr Simkin B-n-r-d.)

* A special kind of tricorne.

Highland Dress

The famous costume of the Scottish Highlander – philabeg (little kilt), plaid and jacket – took its present form in the 1720s. We cannot claim to have covered the period if we ignore it.

Before that time the belted plaid alone composed male Highland dress – a very large plaid folded in pleats and belted round the waist to form a single all-purpose garment. The lower part hung to the knee like a modern kilt; the rest either hung down like a longer skirt, or was twisted round the torso, or else wrapped round the wearer so that at a pinch he could manage with no other garment. About 1725 an Englishman working in the Highlands had the idea of cutting it in two, sewing the pleats permanently into the lower part to make a modern kilt and using the rest independently. The idea spread fast and for a long time both versions were in use. Now the earlier is obsolete. The flat bonnet and sporran continued in use as before. The latter, hanging from the belt in front, had since the Middle Ages been a convenient purse to carry food, ammunition, etc.

After the Jacobite rising of 1745 a harsh law forbade the

wearing of Highland dress – only the Highland regiments of the British Army could wear it legally. This proscription continued less than forty years (repealed 1782) and thereafter the dress was worn again, but less universally than before.

Scottish women's dress was always less distinctive. Just a large tartan plaid worn above the dress and wrapped over head and body, which could be belted at the waist and was fastened with a brooch at the breast. But by the sixteenth century fashion was already tempting women of rank and wealth to leave off the tartan.

Children's Dress

Throughout our two centuries children were dressed like their parents, in adult clothes made small. Our period closes just before the first style specially designed for children appeared.

Doubtless children's everyday clothes had always been made of strong stuff, however. Little girls usually wore aprons, for obvious reasons; and toddlers would have streamers, rather like long sleeves hanging from their shoulders, which functioned as leading reins.

Only one thing was special to children – the dresses worn by little boys for their first six or seven years. They were dressed exactly like their sisters, and only hats and toys indicated the sex of a little child. It was a red letter day when a boy was breeched, terrifically important to him. Thomas Nashe remarks that 'a boy new breeched . . . leaps and danceth for joy'. Afterwards he dressed like father, complete with a small sword on formal occasions.

Babies and tiny tots wore biggins, close fitting caps that covered their heads. They were all swaddled in the first months of life, but at the end of our period advanced thinkers were beginning to discard the swaddling bands.

Colour Plates

1 Lady of quality and Boy, c. 1550

2 **English Lady and Spanish Nobleman, c. 1553**

3 Dutch and English Ladies, c. 1557

4 Lady in Spanish farthingale, c. 1560

5 English Gentleman and Spanish Lady, c. 1560-72

French, 1570

French, 1575

English, 1575

English, 1585

English, 1583

6 **Men's head and neck wear of the sixteenth century**

7 **Young Lady and Gentleman, c. 1564-9**

8 German fashions of the sixteenth century

9 Spanish Nobleman and Lady, c. 1565

10 Spanish Princess in a farthingale, c. 1571

11 A German masquerade costume, c. 1578

12 **Fashionable German Lady and Gentleman, c. 1580**

13 **Going to the Ball—German style, c. 1580**

Man's cap, 1570

Slashed doublet and
bombasted trunk
hose, 1577

Boy's full Venetian trunk hose
with sleeveless jerkin, 1574

Buff jerkin with
ribbon points, 1580

14 Doublet and jerkin fashions, c. 1570-80

15 Spanish Lady in jewelled gown, and Nobleman, c. 1590

French, 1572

French, 1570

Dutch, 1587

Spanish, 1585

English, 1573

16 Ladies' head and neck wear of the sixteenth century

17 An Elizabethan fashion, c. 1592

Venetian fashion, 1581

French fashion, 1584

Young lady's fashion, 1564

A white widow costume, 1550s

Wearing the bum roll, 1590

18 The fashionable shapes of the sixteenth century

19 **Young Prince and Princess,** c. **1614**

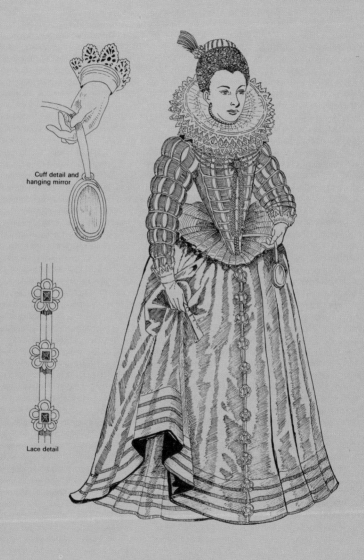

Cuff detail and
hanging mirror

Lace detail

20 French fashion of the early seventeenth century

21 English fashions, c. 1616

Large cocked hat with
feather decoration, 1620

Doublet with panes and
winged sleeves, 1620–25

Falling ruff with tasselled
band-strings, 1620–30

Linen stockings
embroidered in silk, 1620

22 The doublet, falling ruff and other fashions, c. 1620-30

23 **A Gentleman in armour, and a fashionable Gentleman**, c. **1625**

24-25 Spanish Royal Equestrians, c. 1629

26 **German Soldier and Boy, c. 1628**

27 **Lady in black, and Boy, c. 1628**

28 German Soldier Musicians—fifer and drummer, c. 1628

29　Velázquez's Spanish Lady, c. 1630

30 **German Officer and Lady in riding habit, c. 1630**

31 Lady and Gentleman going to a wedding, c. 1630

32 **Lady and Gentleman in Court dress, c. 1630**

33 Cavalier Officer and Lady, c. 1630

34 **The wearing of the cloak, c. 1630**

35 **Musketeer and country Girl in pattens, c. 1633**

36 **Nobleman and Boy in hunting attire, c. 1635**

37 English Earl and Lady in Court dress, c. 1635

Dutch, 1632

English, 1645

French, 1630

Dutch, 1610

German, 1630

English, 1616

Dutch, 1660

38 Ladies' hair and head-dress fashions, c. 1610-60

39 **Countess and Child, c. 1640**

40 Merchants' Wives, English and Dutch fashions, c. 1640

41 Lady in 'chaperone' and mask, with Nobleman, c. 1640

42 **Country Gentleman and his Wife, c. 1640**

43 **Children of a Royal Family, c. 1641**

44 Ladies in summer fashions, c. 1643

45 English Lady in furs and mask, and a Dutch Lady, c. 1643

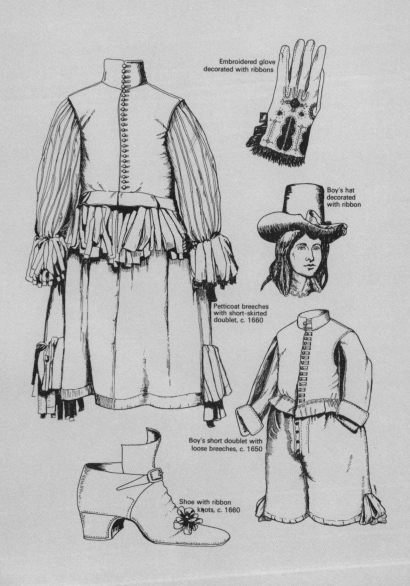

Embroidered glove decorated with ribbons

Boy's hat decorated with ribbon

Petticoat breeches with short-skirted doublet, c. 1660

Boy's short doublet with loose breeches, c. 1650

Shoe with ribbon knots, c. 1660

46 · **Petticoat and loose breeches fashion, mid-seventeenth century**

47 **Autumnal fashions of a Lady and Child, c. 1650**

48 A young Spanish Princess, c. 1659

49 **Dutch Nobleman and his Wife, c. 1660**

50 Dutch Gentleman in petticoat breeches with Lady, c. 1665

51 Fashionable Lady in evening dress, c. 1668

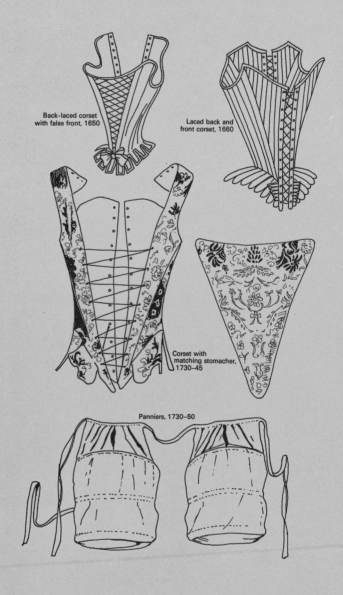

Back-laced corset
with false front, 1650

Laced back and
front corset, 1660

Corset with
matching stomacher,
1730–45

Panniers, 1730–50

52 Corsets and panniers of the seventeenth and eighteenth centuries

53 **Officer in 'bucket boots' with a Lady, c. 1675**

54 French Farmer and Milkmaid in country costume, c. 1678

Boy's costume, 1564

Spanish boy, 1575

Girl's dress with virago sleeves
and lace collar, 1632

Young boy's costume, 1560–80

Girl with round-eared cap, 1740

55 Children's fashions of the sixteenth to eighteenth centuries

56 **Officer and his Lady, c. 1678**

57 **French Officer in 'bloomer' style with Lady, c. 1682**

58 **Fashionable Gentleman and a peasant Girl, c. 1684**

59 **Palace Guard Officer and Lady with a 'fontange', c. 1693**

60 **Gentleman of quality and a fashionable Lady, c. 1694**

61 **Nobleman and his Son, c. 1695**

Shoe with patten, 1730–50

Silk shoe, 1660–80.

Buckled shoe, 1730–50

Satin slipper with laced frill, 1730

Ladies' embroidered slipper, 1700

Embroidered silk pantofle worn by both men and women, 1714

Satin mule, 1660–80

62 Late seventeenth- and early eighteenth-century shoe fashions

63 **Officer with snuffbox, and Lady, c. 1698**

64 French General with Lady in riding habit, c. 1704

65 **Gentleman in morning gown, c. 1712**

66 **Officer and his Lady, c. 1720**

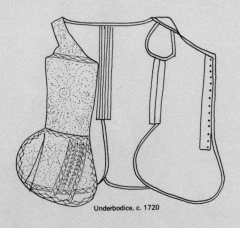

Underbodice, c. 1720

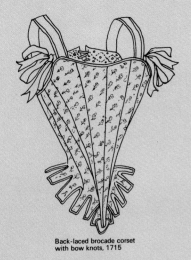

Back-laced brocade corset
with bow knots, 1715

Front-laced damask corset, 1725

67 Early eighteenth-century corset fashions

68 Lady in riding habit wearing a Steinkirk cravat, c. 1720

69 Fashionable Gentlemen of quality, c. 1725

70 **Officer in armoured breastplate with Lady, c. 1727**

71 Lady wearing a mantua, and Gentleman in redingote, c. 1729

72-73 **Ladies in the voluminous 'robe battante', c. 1729**

74 Lady and Gentleman in Highland costume, c. 1745

75 Lady in quilted petticoat, c. 1745

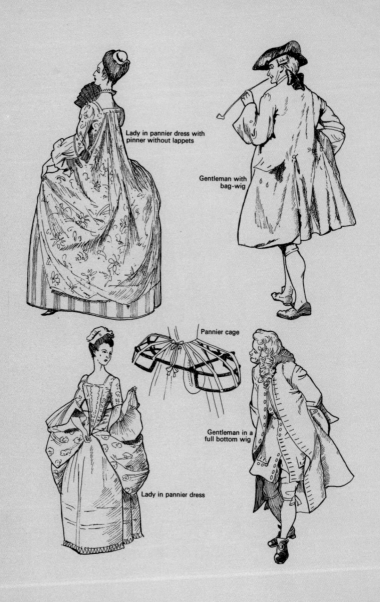

Lady in pannier dress with pinner without lappets

Gentleman with bag-wig

Pannier cage

Gentleman in a full bottom wig

Lady in pannier dress

76 Early eighteenth-century fashions

77 **Fashionable Lady with embroidered robings, c. 1750**

78 **Madame de Pompadour, c. 1755**

79 Guards Officer with Lady, c. 1758

80 **Lady in 'bergère' hat with Gentleman Officer, c. 1760**

Plate Descriptions

1 Lady of quality and Boy, c. 1550

The lady is dressed in the English style of the period. The bodice was tight-fitting with a square yoke of darker colour, and had a high neck with a Medici collar. The *décolletage* was covered by a partlet, a kind of stomacher. The high collar was closed by a gold jewelled 'choker' with a pendant hanging to the yoke. The sleeves were funnel shaped, close-fitting at the top, then expanding to a wide opening from the elbow, with a large cuff turning back to the elbow bend in front, and falling down to some length at the back. The undersleeves were trimmed with embroidered edgings and aiglets which, when fastened, closed the undersleeves. The skirt, in the Spanish farthingale style, had the forepart matching the undersleeves; the overskirt being the same as the bodice. The headwear was the English version of the French hood, made on a stiff base and worn close-fitting towards the back of the head. It was curved forward to end just over the ears on either side, and the back raised into a horse-shoe shape. The falling folds at the back, usually stiffened, could be turned up and laid flat across the top, protruding slightly over the forehead. Worn this way it protected the face from the sun and was called a 'bongrace'. The hair which was exposed had a centre parting and was so arranged as to be full at the temples. Suspended from the narrow girdle by a gold chain was a 'Book of Hours', although many accessories, such as mirrors, purses, muffs, etc., could be worn.

The boy, dressed in the fashion of the adults, wore the padded doublet. Although a little longer than in the previous period, it still retained the bulky appearance; the waistline being just above the hips. The doublet, sleeves and trunk hose were slashed, revealing patches of the chemise worn underneath. Following the fashion of his elders, a cod-piece was worn. The jacket followed the shape of the doublet. The collar was turned down flat on the shoulders. In most cases the jacket was worn open, revealing the doublet. The sleeves, if worn, were slashed from just below the shoulder to just below the elbow. The small bonnet with a full pleated crown was worn with a bunch of feathers decorating one side. The shoes, matching the rest of the outfit, were decorated with slashings. A small 'hanger' type sword was worn suspended from the girdle by leather slings.

2 English Lady and Spanish Nobleman, c. 1553

The lady is wearing a high-necked, close-fitting gown with a small closed-all-round ruff. The bodice was close-fitting and fairly rigid, with the waistline sloping to a deep V-shape point in front, fastening down the left side by hooks. A gored skirt expanded in a funnel shape without folds from the small tight waist to the ground. This shape depended on the underlying Spanish farthingale—an underskirt distended by circular hoops called 'bents' made from wire, wood or whalebone. The sleeves had a welt which surrounded the armhole and formed a small wing effect. Known as the 'bishop' style, these sleeves were full from the shoulder to the wrist, finishing in a tight cuff from which extended a small wrist ruff. A girdle of narrow cord or metal chain surrounded the waist from which hung a pomander on a cord or chain. The close-fitting coif covered the hair and ears and was fastened under the chin; it was made from linen or other suchlike material. Over this was worn the 'bongrace', popular from 1530 to 1615. This was usually made from stiffened velvet, oblong in shape and worn

A gold pomander

flat on the head. One end formed a brim effect over the forehead, the other part fell down the back of the head to the shoulders, thus protecting the face and neck from the sun.

The man wears a Spanish style which by 1750 began to decline in popularity in Europe. The body of the doublet, slightly formed in the peascod belly style, was well padded; the point or girdlestead was deep and curved downwards. A high-standing collar was edged with a turned-down border fashioned in pickadils to support a ruff. This plate shows only the short chemise collar extended. The doublet sleeves were close-fitting to the wrist ending in short wrist ruffs. The trunk hose had long slashes and were also ornamented with the fashionable cod-piece. The gown was faced and lined with fur; the puffed-out shoulder sleeves had lace decoration. The length of the gown reached just above the knees, and was usually worn open. Slashed shoes of soft leather, silk or velvet were worn.

3   Dutch and English Ladies, c. 1557

The lady on the right is wearing a gown. This overgarment was worn on formal occasions, and also for warmth, over the bodice and skirt. The loose-bodied gown had a high neck which was surmounted by a small ruff. Short, puffed-out shoulder sleeves to elbow length revealed the straight sleeves of the bodice, which ended in wrist ruffs. Fitting close to the shoulders, the gown, when fastened from the neck to the waist, formed a conical shape to the ground, leaving an inverted V-shape opening from the waist to the hem, so revealing the dress beneath. The gown was decorated with broad guards of velvet. The headwear worn was the popular French hood. Short-cuffed leather gloves were often carried.

The lady on the left is wearing a Dutch-style hood, or 'cornet', with lappets. This was made of lawn, linen and white gauze or muslin with wire frames. The one-piece gown, worn over the bodice and skirt, fitted the figure at the waist then overhung the hips; the full, gathered skirt falling to the ground. The French full sleeves expanded into wide turned-back cuffs, showing the lining of quilted velvet. Broad bands or guards of velvet decorated the sleeves. A distinctive feature of the costume was the full, sheer *guimpe* or chemise which appeared through the square-shaped *décolletage*. The bodice of the gown was open from the neck to the waist. A jewelled girdle was worn, which had a long end hanging in front and a tassel at the end.

4 Lady in Spanish far-thingale, c. 1560

This portrait of a Lady after Federigo Zucchero, shows a dress with the bodice in a low, square neckline and a partlet front. The standing collar was open in front. Around the neck, beads were worn, high at the top and then falling down the front. The bodice was tight-fitting, tapering to a short point at the waist. The oversleeves were puffed at the top and short enough to reveal the long, tight undersleeves which reached to the wrists, and ended in small ruffs. The Spanish farthingale skirt, also known as the 'verdingale', was elaborately embroidered, as was the forepart which matched the long undersleeves. The girdle followed the curved waistline down the front, and then hung down almost to the hem-line. The hair, visible under the caul, was

Lady wearing a caul

parted in the centre. The caul was a close-fitting cap reticulated in gold thread and decorated with pearls and precious jewels; it covered the back of the head. Ladies invariably carried a scented handkerchief.

5 English Gentleman and Spanish Lady, c. 1560–72

The lady is wearing a court bonnet decorated with pearls and drooping ostrich feathers. This was a moderately deep, full-crowned cap pleated onto a head-band; it had a narrow brim. This bonnet was worn over a jewelled caul, and was known as a 'taffeta pipkin'. The bodice of the dress was corseted, coming down to a deep point in front with the bell-shaped hoop of Spanish origin. This bodice was close-fitting down to the waist, then expanded over the hips; the gathered skirt falling in stiff folds to the ground. The high-necked collar was surrounded by a medium-sized, closed-all-round ruff. The sleeves were full, hanging down almost to the hem, and worn over undersleeves of brocaded satin with lace edgings at the cuffs, forming wrist ruffs. Gowns of this type were usually velvet. They were ornamented with ribbon points on the sleeves and down the front, which, when not fastened, revealed the brocaded underskirt or petticoat which matched the undersleeves. The bodice was ornamented down the centre and down either side with encrustations of jewels. Matching these was the girdle belt with a hanging chain supporting a pomander.

The gentleman wears Venetian breeches or slops, which were voluminous with looped borders in pickadils at the knees. The jerkin was tied by points, but usually fastened only at the chest and then allowed to open so as to reveal the doublet beneath. Stray points fastened the breeches to the undersurface of the doublet which had modified trunk sleeves. The high-necked doublet had a medium-sized ruff, closed all round; the band strings were

tied and concealed. The doublet in this Venetian style was padded at the stomach, giving the appearance of a peascod. The hair was fairly short. Beards were very fashionable throughout this period, i.e. from 1570 to 1600. Hand ruffs, made like small neck ruffs, were usually worn.

6 Men's head and neckwear of the sixteenth century

The head and neckwear fashions of the sixteenth century altered very little; the hair remained close cut, and beards and moustaches were worn in varying degrees of fullness.

Top left The French fashion of the 1570s was the 'toques rondes' or round bonnet of striped velvet. The low crown was pleated onto a narrow, rolled-up brim. In the centre of the front was a silk rosette of pearls and semi-precious stones, decorated with small ostrich feather tips. The bonnet was worn towards the back of the head. Short hair and a marquisetto beard were worn. Fashionable then were pearl earrings for men. Around the neck was a large cartwheel ruff.

Top right The French toque of velvet from c. 1575. The crown was heightened by wire supports, and was pleated onto a very narrow brim. The bonnet was decorated with a hat band of semi-precious jewels, with feathers at the side, and was worn at a tilt. The fashionable short hair and beard were worn, also pearl ear-rings. A medium-sized ruff closed all round was worn.

Centre The English style of *c.* 1575. The bonnet had a very high, bag-like crown stiffened with buckram and wire, the whole being pleated onto a medium narrow brim. The brim was slightly cocked to one side. The hat was trimmed around the hat band with braid and buttons and a short feather to the side or in the centre. The hair was short and the face clean shaven. A medium-sized, closed ruff surrounded the neck. English men did not often wear pearl ear-rings.

Bottom left The English style of *c.* 1585 was the low crowned, beret-type bonnet of velvet. The pleated crown was attached to a narrow, drooping all-round brim. The bonnet was decorated with a single jewel ornament in the centre front, and worn over a velvet coif or under-cap. A

moustache and forked beard were worn. A closed ruff encircled the neck.

Bottom right The English fashion of 1583. The high-crowned 'copotain' type hat was made of beaver. The conical crown was attached to a moderately wide brim which was cocked slightly to one side and decorated on the underside with small interlinking gold rings. A large ostrich feather was added for further ornamentation. The hair was short and a full moustache and beard were worn. A small closed ruff surrounded the neck.

7 Young Lady and Gentleman, c. 1564–9

The young lady is wearing a deep-pointed bodice with a low, square neckline. The partlet, or filled-in part, matched the underskirt in design. Around the high neck was worn a small ruff. The short, puffed-out sleeves were worn over long, close undersleeves which matched the underskirt and partlet. The border of the neckline and down the front of the open skirt was similar to the pickadils. The headwear was the very popular 'taffeta pipkin' The deep crown was pleated onto a head band; the brim was flat and narrow. The hat was decorated with ostrich tips and aigrettes.

The young gentleman wears a doublet with a high-standing collar and a small ruff above. The doublet was closed down the front from the top of the collar to the waist, by a row of small buttons fairly close together. The skirt, which reached the hips, was decorated at the waist with pickadils (scalloped borders). A narrow belt and sling was worn around the waist, and supported a sword on the left side. The cloak with hanging sleeves was possibly made of silk brocade and was lined and edged with fur. It had a standing collar reaching down to the bottom of the trunk hose, which were paned. Panes were long thin strips of material which ran parallel and were joined to the hose at the waist and at the ends. The tailored stockings were quite plain. The pumps had rounded toes and were closed at the ankles. The bonnet was trimmed around the edge and decorated with a plume on one side. Short perfumed gloves were carried.

8 German fashions of the sixteenth century

German fashion of the sixteenth century was a slow transformation, and the tight, stiff Spanish styles came gradually.

The man's doublet was padded, slightly bombast, and close-fitting. It had a high neck and a tight waist which was slightly pointed in front. The doublet was fastened from the high neck, to the waist by a close row of buttons. The high neck concealed the top buttons under a small ruff. The skirt was short and expanded over the padded pluderhose. The trunk sleeves, which were wide at the shoulders and narrowed to the wrist, were closed by a small wrist ruff. Pluderhose were very baggy breeches popular with the Germans; they were adopted from the mercenary soldiers of the previous

German hat style, 1580–90

period. These breeches were made from two pairs, one inside the other. The outer pair were made up from four to six vertical panes or slashes, about fifteen centimetres in width. The inner pair were made of thin silk, or 'rasch' using some forty to sixty metres, which was arranged in thick pleats round the body to produce the bulky bagginess required. The hose were then divided into strips and the bottom edge of the bagginess was attached to the lower edge of the outer garment and the lining. The lining, being tighter than the hose, came only to the knee, so the baggy 'pullings-out' fell from the thigh to the knee. Tailored stockings were made separately from the pluderhose; cross gartering was used to tie the stockings. The garter was tied below the knee in front, the ends taken back behind the knee, then brought forward above the knee where they ended in a bow on the front. The shoes were narrow and pointed at the toe; they enclosed the foot up to the ankle. They were slashed and made from soft leather, silk or velvet. The cloak was about mid-thigh in length, and had a standing collar decorated with small pickadils along the edge. The 'barrett' hat worn was low crowned, lightly padded and had a stiff broad brim. Small triangular pieces were cut out, then joined by narrow ribbon so that the brim stood in a perpendicular position. Feathers hung around the brim. The hair was short and a pickdevant beard with the brushed-up moustache was worn.

The lady of fashion of this period wears the close-fitting bodice with the high neckline, which was encircled with a small, closed neck-ruff. The bodice was closed in front from neck to waistline. The skirts were gathered at the high waistline and were full and pleated to the ground. The bodice had a puffed-out shoulder sleeve gathered onto a band round the arm just above the elbow, then continued with a close-fitting sleeve to the wrist, ending in a hand ruff. The short, jerkin-type jacket stood stiffly away from the body and was trimmed with a wide fur collar from shoulder to hem. A 'barrett' cap, made of stiffened cloth laid over a framework of wire, was worn covering the hair. Aprons were worn as elegant accessories, especially in this period.

9 Spanish Nobleman and Lady, c. 1565

The lady illustrated wears a loose-bodied gown which fitted the shoulders, then hung down in stiff folds to the ground. The gown had a standing collar with rounded corners, and was tied in front. The separate ruff worn with the high standing collar was closed all round and was of medium size. Although usually worn open, the gown was often closed from neck to hem with ties. Sometimes a narrow girdle fastened the gown at the waist. The sleeves were close-fitting to the wrist and finished with a deep, turned-back cuff of lace. A small muff hung from the girdle on a ribbon or cord. A reticulated caul was worn which covered the back of the head, leaving the forehead uncovered; the hair was turned back over a pad or 'palisadoe', to give fullness at the temples.

The gentleman wears a close-fitting, deep-waisted, sleeveless jerkin which buttoned down the front from the high collar to the waistline. The long skirt expanded over the bombasted,

slashed trunk hose and reached just below the fork. The exposed sleeves of the doublet were close-fitting and finished at the wrists with ruffs which matched the short, neck ruff. The cloak was sleeveless and hung down just below the trunk hose. The tailored stockings were cut on the cross and called nether-stocks. Shoes were made in various materials such as leather, silk, brocade and velvet. The uppers were usually slashed or pinked in symmetrical designs. The court bonnet was made in velvet or cloth and trimmed with jewelled ornaments and a small feather plume. It was usually worn at an angle with a backward tilt. Short, fine leather gloves with a contrasting colour at the wrists were worn. Walking

Spanish sword

sticks of wood, usually long with decorative metal knobs, were often carried.

10 Spanish Princess in a farthingale, c. 1571

The illustration shows a Spanish-style gown, an over-garment for warmth and formal occasions, which was worn over the bodice and skirt. The close-bodied gown fitted the figure to the waist then extended over the hips. Fitting close to the shoulders it fell spreading outwards to the ground, leaving an inverted V-shaped opening in front from the waist to the hem. This is shown closed by ribbons and points. The Spanish far-thingale, or verdingale, was an underskirt distended by circular hoops, each hoop increasing in circumference finally forming a wide circle at the feet, so producing a funnel shape. This farthingale skirt was gored so that it sloped stiffly outwards from the waist to the ground, making a smooth flat surface without folds, and was called a 'round kirtle'. The gown had a standing collar, tied or buttoned in front. Long sham hanging sleeves, brocaded and silk lined, fastened at just below elbow level by ribbon and jewelled points. A large opening then revealed the undersleeve of the undergarment made of batiste with lace ribbon loops. A small ruff was attached to the high collar of the chemise. The lady wore the small Mary Stuart hood-type of head-dress made of lawn or similar material and trimmed with lace and jewellery. Gloves were worn, similar to those worn by the men. They were made of scented leather and called 'sweet gloves'. A handker-chief of lawn, trimmed with lace was carried.

Handkerchief detail

11 A German masquerade costume, c. 1578

The illustration shows a fashionable gentleman with the added accessories of a full face-mask and lute. The doublet was usually worn over a chemise or shirt, and was close-fitting, tight-waisted and slightly pointed in front. The body of the doublet was lightly padded. It had a standing collar topped with small, horizontal stiffened tabs, called pickadils, which could be used either as ornamentation or as supports for the medium or small ruffs. The doublet was fastened from the collar to the waist with a row of buttons down the front. The skirt was very short, almost concealed by the narrow, leather girdle belt. The trunk sleeves were wide at the shoulders and narrowed to a closed wrist which ended in a wrist ruff. A narrow wing welt encircled the armhole. The trunk hose (pluderhose) were often called 'plunderhose' as these voluminous nether garments made good hiding places for stolen or plundered goods. They were made from two garments, the outer being vertical strips of material, the inner being made from many metres of silken material attached to a lining, then pulled out to hang down to the knees. The linings were arranged so that they could be hitched up over the sword belt giving a baggy effect across the middle. The long, full stockings made of material, were fastened on with a ribbon sash; this was placed below the knee in front, the ends passing to the back giving a cross-twist behind the knee, then forward above the knee and finishing in a large ribbon knot in front. The shoes were shaped to a blunt point at the toe, were narrow and encased the foot up to the ankle. They were slashed and ornamented and usually made from soft leathers, but velvet and silks were still popular. The French-style bonnet was worn. Made of velvet, the high crown was heightened with wire and stiffened slightly with buckram. The crown was pleated onto a narrow brim. The hat band was either twisted silk or formed by jewels, and the hat decoration was usually a plume of feathers either in centre front or at the side. The wearing of masks was very popular. Masks were made and worn for many occasions, not only for carnivals and masquerades, but also for every day use. They were made in various materials such as silk, satin and taffeta, and lined in silk or skin.

12 Fashionable German Lady and Gentleman, c. 1580

This German style worn by the lady, was a variation of the gown overgarment which was worn over the bodice and skirt. The loose-bodied gown fitted the shoulders and fell in set folds from the waist to the ground in a funnel shape, broadest at the hem. The front was open in an inverted V-shape from neck to hem, revealing the dress beneath. The gown was untrained, and the standing collar with rounded edges was left open. The gown had short, puffed sleeves with a 'kick-up' at the shoulders. They ended just above the elbow where they were gathered onto a band. A small, closed frill was attached to the high collar of the bodice of the undergarment. Narrow, wrist frills were attached to the close-fitting, long undergarment sleeves. An apron was worn as an elegant accessory to the walking-out costume. The re-ticulated caul, which closely resembled a hair-net, was lined with silk and was worn covering the back of the head. It could be worn with or without a hat. The hat shown is the popular 'taffeta pipkin' made with a medium-size crown pleated on to a head-band. It had a narrow brim and was decorated with a feather.

The gentleman wears a close-fitting doublet which had a round waist and was worn over the skirt. The body of the doublet was padded and stiffened with canvas to achieve the peascod belly effect—a popular Dutch fashion. The collar was high at the back, curving out slightly in front. A small closed ruff was also worn. The full-padded trunk sleeves, wide but narrowing to the wrist, finished with a narrow hand ruff. The sleeves were slashed. The doublet was fastened by a close row of buttons from the top of the collar to the waist. The plain skirt was very short and narrow, little more than a border, yet deep enough to conceal the points which supported the trunk hose. The front edges were cut to form a small inverted V-shape. The trunk hose sloped outwards from the waist, swelling with the bombast stuffing to about mid-thigh, and were decorated with panes—gay coloured linings drawn through gaps. Separate stockings were worn and these were either cross-gartered or just tied under the knees. The shoes were bluntly pointed, without heels and made from various materials such as leather, velvet, or cloth; the tops were slashed. The cloak worn was hip length and had a standing collar.

13 Going to the Ball— German style, c. 1580

At this period, Spanish ladies' fashions were introduced into Germany, and the fashion of wearing one dress over another was the considered vogue. In this plate the underdress had a long close-fitting bodice of a quilted material. The overdress fitted only at the shoulders and gradually increased in width downwards, following the contours of the Spanish farthingale which supported the heavy dress. The gown was open down the front, but could, in the event of inclement weather or otherwise, be fastened from neck to hem, or to the waist only. The sleeves were the long, tubular type of hanging sleeve with a large opening revealing the upper underbodice sleeves. They were joined at the elbow, then opened again to reveal the lower part of the underbodice sleeves. The gown was decorated with broad guards or bands of braid. Cartwheel ruffs of large dimensions were now in fashion. They were closed all round; the band strings were concealed from view. These ruffs were made of linen, and were starched and ironed for stiffness. They were supported by a wire framework called an 'underpropper'. The headwear worn was a coif—a one-piece hat with a seam along the top, cut with a point over the forehead, the sides curving away. It was made from linen and decorated with cut feathers. The hair had a centre parting and was turned back over pads giving a fullness at the temples. A fan, made of feathers radiating from a jewelled handle, was carried.

The gentleman wears the 'copotain' type of headwear which had a conical-shaped, high crown and a narrow brim ornamented with ostrich feather tips. He wore the fashionable

'Copotain' hat

marquisetto moustache and beard. His hair was short and brushed-up stiffly from the temples and forehead. This was often aided by gum. The hair of the back of the head was also short. The bombasted doublet was pointed in the front, and was without skirts. It was fastened down the centre with a single row of buttons from the neck to the waistline. The cloak, which ended just below the waist, had a turned-down collar which merged into narrow revers in front, decorated with guards of braid. The trunk hose, worn with full stockings, were short and pumpkin-shaped, and bombasted with padding to give fullness. The shoes were full to the ankle and were slashed in the fashionable mode.

14 Doublet and jerkin fashions, c. 1570–80

The doublet was worn over the chemise or skirt and was still an indispensable garment at this time.

Top right The Italian doublet style closely fitted the body from the neck to just below the waist, where it finished with a short skirt of tabs. The doublet was boned and padded, with the front edge curving outwards to a point below the waist, giving a slight peascod belly effect. It was slashed and pinked in design. The high-standing collar was edged with pickadils—short tabs turned out horizontally to support the lace ruff. The ruff was folded into figure-of-eight shapes and surrounded the neck. The doublet was buttoned down the centre from neck to waist. The armholes were encircled with slightly padded, crescent-shaped welts or, as they were called, 'wings'. The sleeves were long and tight-fitting, and like the doublet, slashed and pinked in design. They ended with a wrist ruff of lace. The waist was encircled by a narrow belt with slings to support the sword. The trunk hose were bombasted to give extra fullness.

Top left A man's night cap.

Bottom left The boy wears the sleeveless jerkin over a close-fitting doublet. The jerkin, which was tight to the body and similar in style to the doublet, had double wings made from small pickadil tabs. Around the high-standing collar was a closed neck ruff. The close-fitting sleeves of the doublet ended in wrist ruffs which matched the ruff at the neck. The trunk hose were in the full Venetian style, pear-shaped and closed below the knees.

Bottom right A buff jerkin which was cut in the same style as a doublet, with winged welts. Around the waist were the silk ribbon bows and points which supported the trunk hose.

15 Spanish Lady in jewelled gown, and Nobleman, c. 1590

The gentleman wears the high-necked, bombasted doublet of the Spanish style, slightly peascod, with a short skirt. The doublet was slashed, pinked and embroidered and had a centre fastening with buttons from the neck to the waist. The standing collar was edged at the top with pickadils. The short skirt was flared out over the padded trunk hose, concealing the points which joined the trunk hose to the doublet. The sleeves were close-fitting to the wrist, ending in small wrist ruffs. Like the doublet, the sleeves were also slashed and pinked. On the shoulders were narrow wings covering the joins of the sleeves to the doublet. The trunk hose were shaped like padded pumpkins and reached down to about mid-thigh. They were often called 'Spanish kettledrums' and were paned for decoration. By this period the cod-piece had diminished in size—this was the front fastening of the trunk hose often used as a pocket. The stockings were tailored to individual requirements. The footwear was made to fit close to the ankles, ending in two small tongues; the uppers were slashed and pinked. The short, hip-length cloak was collarless, designed to fit the shoulders and flare out over the doublet. The hat was tall with a flat top and a narrow curled brim, decorated with a narrow jewelled hat band and a feather plume. The hair was worn rather short. A rapier-type sword was carried, attached to a waist belt.

The lady wears the corseted bodice with a deep point. The

Gentleman's slashed shoe

heavy, jewel encrusted, long stomacher-front dipped to a point over the stiff Spanish farthingale skirt. Full trunk-type sleeves with large, laced wrist cuffs of the under-bodice were revealed under the huge hanging sleeves. The gown fitted the shoulders and the figure to the waist, then expanded over the hips and fell stiffly to the ground forming a large funnel shape. The gown fastened from the high-standing collar to the hem with large jewelled buttons and loops. Above the hanging sleeves were shoulder wings. The width of the fashionable lace ruff had reached enormous dimensions. It was made of fine lace and was both starched and wired. The brocade gown was heavily embroidered and ornamented with encrustations of jewels. A narrow jewelled sash encircled the waist,

and from which a pomander was suspended. The hair was drawn off the face, waved or curled and arranged over wire frames; it was decorated with pearls. A folding fan was carried.

16 Ladies' head and neck wear of the sixteenth century

Top left c. 1572. French fashion of a tall-crowned hat with a narrow brim, decorated with silk twists and a back ribbon, usually made from velvet. This hat was worn over a caul which covered the back of the head.

Top right A lower crowned, beret-type hat decorated with jewellery and feathers. French *c.* 1570.

Centre The Mary Stuart hood, 1550–1630. A small hood of lawn with the front border wired to form a wide curve with a dip above the centre of the forehead. The sides were brought forward, ending over the ears; the hair was visible at the temples. This Dutch style was worn with an under-cap.

Bottom left c. 1585. Spanish style, tall-crowned, brimless hat, decorated with jewellery around the lower part, and ornamented with high-standing ostrich feathers fastened with precious stones.

Bottom right c. 1573. English style, tall-crowned hat with a small turned-up brim and a jewelled hat band. It was decorated with the popular large ostrich feather. The hat was worn over an under-cap.

17 An Elizabethan fashion, c. 1592

The bodice of this simple, heavily-padded dress was close-fitting with a long-fronted stomacher dipping in a deep point to the stiffened basque of the French farthingale. The basque, of the same material as the flounced tub-shaped skirt, concealed the hard line of the exclusive fashion of the wheel farthingale. The trunk sleeves were full at the top and tapered to the wrists. This type of sleeve was sometimes called 'demi-cannon'. The wrists were finished with short, turn-back cuffs of lace. Behind these sleeves hung huge false hanging sleeves which reached the ground. The stomacher, an inverted triangular piece used as a fill-in for the bodice, was positioned in such a way that the upper straight edge formed a low square *décolletage* across the front. It was made of the same material as the dress, and stiffened with buckram or canvas. The bodice was joined to the stomacher by hidden ties or pins. The low *décolletage* was finished off with white lace, bordering the straight edge across the front, and a lace, fan-shaped ruff. This type of ruff was arranged around the back and sides of the *décolletage*, spreading out fan-wise at the back of the head. Although used mostly for formal occasions, this ruff was generally worn by unmarried women, sometimes to the extreme fashion of displaying their breasts with a lowering of the *décolletage*. Behind this open, white lace ruff was a diaphanous wing collar on a wired head-rail which reached the top of the head in height; this was trimmed with jewels. Long strands of pearls hung down the front of the dress to the stiffened basque of the farthingale. The hair was decorated with pearls and a jewelled head ornament. A folding fan was attached to the waist by a ribbon cord. Gloves with tabbed cuffs were also worn, or simply carried as an accessory.

18 The fashionable shapes of the sixteenth century

The forms of ladies' silhouettes varied considerably during this period.

Top left The Venetian style—a most exaggerated fashion of bombast and padding, and fantastic hair shapes.

Top right The French verdingale which was formed by a large hoop at hip level tilted down in the front. This dress had wide, exaggerated shoulders with large stuffed, sausage-like sleeves.

Centre The tight-laced corselet—German style of 1564.

Bottom left The white widow's 'weeds' or dress—a French style of the 1550s.

Bottom right The Dutch fashion of the 1590s to 1600s showing the wearing of the 'bum-roll' or roll farthingale, formed by padded rolls stuffed with bombast or cotton.

19 Young Prince and Princess, c. 1614

The young lady wears the French wheel farthingale. This wheel shape was made from whalebone or wire covered with material. The lower body acted as the hub of the wheel, with the dress expanding around the hips in a downward tilt at the front and an exaggerated upward tilt at the back. The fully-gathered, tub-shaped skirt was worn over this farthingale structure, and fell vertically to the ground in stiff folds. The dress bodice was close-fitting to the body with a low, rounded neckline, and a point at the waist. The waistline was edged with a stiffened frounced skirt or basque which concealed the hard line of the wheel understructure. The sleeves, of the cannon type, were slightly padded, had a 'kick-up' at the shoulders and narrowed to the wrists. Here they were fastened, usually with buttons, and then finished off with a lace turned-back cuff. The low *décolletage* had a lace border across the shoulder and ended in a V-shape at the front. Rising from either side of the *décolletage* a fan-shaped ruff spread out round the back of the head. The hair was crimped and brushed back from the forehead and temples. A caul or small round hat was worn at the back of the head, usually lined with silk and trimmed with jewels and lace. A folding fan was carried. At this period necklaces, bracelets and dresses bedecked with precious and semi-precious stones were still popular.

The boy wears the longer waisted doublet which fitted close to the body, dipping to a sharp point in front. It had a narrow tabbed pointed skirt. The neck was high standing and supported a medium-size, closed-all-round ruff. The doublet was fastened down the front by a close row of buttons. The sleeves were plain and close-fitting, fastening at the wrists by a row of buttons, then ending with a turn-back lace cuff. Wings in the form of protruding welts encircled the shoulders where the sleeves joined the doublet. A highly-decorated narrow sword belt hung around the waist. The trunk hose, of the full-gathered breeches type, were attached to a tight waistband then expanded outwards and downwards. They were padded and stiffened, and turned in at mid-thigh so forming a pumpkin shape. They combined two materials of velvet stripes and panne velvet with braid. The stockings were decorated just below the knees with sashes and ribbon rosettes, which were displayed on the outer side of the legs. The shoes were round-toed,

and had heels made of wood or leather; they were decorated with large shoe roses.

20 French fashion of the early seventeenth century

The lady is wearing a close-fitting bodice with a high neckline. The stomacher came down to the stiffened basque in a sharp point and was slashed, padded, and puckered horizontally to match the sleeves. The trunk sleeves, sometimes called 'cannon sleeves', were wide at the shoulder, narrower at the wrists, and finished with a small turn-back cuff, lace bordered and vandyked. These sleeves were padded and slashed revealing the lining beneath, and stiffened horizontally, giving a honey-comb effect. The neck was enclosed by a large double ruff, which like the cuffs was lace bordered and vandyked. The ruff was supported by pickadils. The wheel-shaped French farthingale fashion was made of wire and covered with silk. It surrounded the waist and had a distinct upward tilt at the back and came down in the front. The frounced skirt of stiffened basque softened the hard shape of the understructure. The skirt was fully gathered at the waist and expanded over the structure to fall in vertical folds to the ground. The skirt was fastened from waist to hem by lace and jewelled buttons, and was often bunched up at the side to reveal the elegant underskirt or petticoat. A small round hat or caul was worn at the back of the head. A small hand mirror, attached at the waist by a ribbon cord, was carried, as was a folding fan.

21　English fashions, c. 1616
The lady wore a high-waisted embroidered jacket, a fashion which was later worn by women for riding. It was an unpadded type of bodice which was close-fitting and flared from the waist in a basque, ending in a straight line around the hips. It was fastened down the front from the neck to the hem with hooks and eyes. The high neckline was round, collar-less, and filled in with a small neck ruff of lace. The sleeves were tight-fitting to the wrist; a broad wing covered the join between the sleeve and shoulder. An embroidered jacket of this type was often worn with loose open gowns and transparent aprons. The form and drape of the skirt

depended on the under-structure, such as petticoats, or the farthingale which was now becoming much smaller. This plate shows a heavily embroidered skirt which gathered at the waist and fell vertically to the ground; it was worn without a farthingale. The hair was brushed-up high on the forehead and temples, then laid over roll pads; the back hair was coiled into a flat bun high at the back of the head, then concealed by a caul made of silk or other material.

The gentleman wears a close-fitting doublet. The front of the doublet curved down in front to a sharp point. Although stiffened with buckram, the padding and bombast of the peascod belly was now out of fashion. The doublet had a high-standing collar and was buttoned in front down to the waist. The sleeves were straight and close-fitting with wings at the shoulders and ended in turn-back lace cuffs. The neck-wear, which was in the transitional form between the ruff and the falling collar, consisted of a standing band made of a transparent material edged with lace; it was held in position around the neck by an 'under-propper'. In this plate an armoured gorget surrounds the neck. The trunk hose were large and heavily padded. The stockings were tailored, and embroidered designs reached almost to the knees. The whole costume was heavily embroidered, braided and lace trimmed. The round-toed shoes tied at the front; the ties being hidden by huge roses. The hair was now slightly longer, almost covering the ears, and small beards and moustaches were becoming very fashionable.

22 The doublet, falling ruff and other fashions, c. 1620–30

Top left A doublet with a high-standing collar, paned on the breast and on the winged sleeves. It had a centre fastening of a close row of buttons. The skirt shows the eyelet holes for attaching the trunk hose by the use of ribbon points.

Top right The popular large cocked hat, decorated with a hat band and large feather. A vandyke beard and moustache were worn.

Bottom left A bird's eye view of the falling ruff, showing the neck piece which was tucked into the high-standing collar of the doublet.

Bottom right Stockings of linen, lightly embroidered in silk.

23 A Gentleman in armour and a fashionable Gentleman, c. 1625

The gentleman on the right wears a high-waisted, loose-fitting doublet, which was almost without stiffening. It dipped to a sharp point in front and had about eight deep squared tabs which overlapped. The two front tabs dipped to a very sharp point and met edge to edge. At the waistline were ribbon points which were the fastenings for the trunk hose. The doublet was fastened from the high-standing collar to the waist by a close row of buttons down the front. The

Cromwellian soldier

breast of the doublet was paned, as was the upper part of the broad projecting winged sleeves. The close-fitting lower part of the sleeves ended in a deep turn-back cuff of lace. Around the neck was worn the standing band called in Spain the 'golillia'. This was made of a transparent material and edged with lace. An underpropper caused the semi-circular collar to stand up round the back of the head. The trunk hose were paned and were worn with stockings. A garter decorated the left leg just below the knee. The shoes had open sides, low heels, rounded toes and were decorated with a ribbon tie. The hair was brushed back from the forehead. It was now longer, falling to just below the ears. 'Vandyke' beards, often waxed, were becoming a very popular mode. Over the arm was carried a draped cloak—an indispensable garment for gentlemen.

The military gentleman on the left wears a full suit of armour over his fashionable clothes. Around his neck he wore a falling band—a wide lace collar which spread horizontally across the shoulders. The lace cuffs were turned back over the armour-covered sleeves. Across the body, from the right shoulder to the left hand side, was a broad lace-decorated baldrick. Breeches were worn stuffed into the top of the boots. The boots, which came well over the knee, were fitted with spurs. From a waist belt and slings hung the sword. The armour of this period was usually described as 'cuirassier's armour' but was little used by the middle of the century. As a defence against fire-arms, armour had become thicker and heavier. To offset this the cuirassier wore only a three-quarter armour reaching to the knees. The *grevières* and *solerets*, defences for the legs and feet, began to be replaced by high buff leather boots. From the waist of the breastplate to the knees were worn long tassets or thigh pieces, made up from many lames. The lower thigh armour was attached to the breast plate by straps or turning pins which fitted into apertures on the tassets. *Pauldrons* and *vambraces*, armour pieces for the arms, were joined into one moveable piece, the elbow protected by overlapping plates. The knees were protected by specially made *genouillières*, knee guards.

24–25 Spanish Royal Equestrians, c. 1629

At the opening of the seventeenth century, Spanish fashion was losing popularity throughout Europe. Spain, however, continued to cling to the style and character of the previous century. Civil costume had always influenced military equipment, and armour was no exception. It was modelled in accordance with the costume in fashion at that period, and was paned and slashed in exactly the same way as were the rich materials used for the costumes.

The man wears the breastplate, or plastron, which was shaped like the doublet of the older style; the peascod, the central ridge or tapul, came down to a deep point at the centre of the waist. Attached to this were the deep hip-length, skirt-like tassets, usually made in two single plates and simulated to look like a series of lames. The guards for the shoulders, *epaulières*, were also made in laminated tasset-form; then came the *brassarts* or *pauldrons* which were arm guards for the upper arms. The *coudières*, or elbow-caps, were used as guards and coverings for the inside of the elbow joints. The lower arms were covered with *avant-bras* or *vambrace* pieces, and strong leather gauntlet-type gloves were worn. The neck guard or *gorgerin* (gorget) was formed by a series of circular pieces of plate carefully connected to cover the throat and to join the helmet to the body armour; but in this costume the neck guard was used to help support the large neck ruff. Across the body from the right shoulder to the left hip was a broad lace-decorated baldrick. The trunk hose, which emerged from the metal skirt, were closely gathered at the waist and fell in folds to a wide base just above the knees. A simple garter just below the knee decorated the long stockings. The hair was short and the vandyke beard and moustache were worn. The tall-crowned hat with the wide brim was decorated with feathers and jewellery.

The lady wears a voluminous, heavily embroidered gown of lavish richness. The high under-bodice was tight to the waist with close-fitting sleeves, and the standing collar of the partlet was surmounted by a large neck ruff. The overgown fitted the shoulders and figure to the waist

and fell in folds spreading outwards, and as this was a ceremonial gown it was also trained.
The *décolletage* was V-shaped,
revealing the bodice. From the
winged shoulders fell long hanging sleeves with openings at
elbow level. The hair was without a parting, and was built over
'palisadoes' or wire raised supports which gave a peak in the
centre and a fullness at the
temples. It was the fashion for
ladies to go bare headed with
only jewellery and feathers as
head adornment.

26 German Soldier and Boy,
    c. 1628

The German soldier wears the
fashion of the day. The high-
waisted doublet was close-fitting
without padding, and was
fastened from the high neck to
the waist with a close row of
buttons. The tabs of the short
skirt were either edge to edge or
slightly overlapping. The close-
fitting sleeves of the lower arms
had short turn-back cuffs; the
upper arms were paned and
finished with a projecting wing.
Around the neck was a broad
falling band. The trunk hose were
worn with cannions and sloped
downwards and outwards in folds

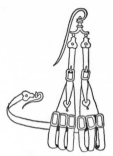

Sword belt, 1628

from a tight waist band. At mid-
thigh the hose were turned in,
and from this wide base came
close-fitting cannions ending just
below the knee. The cannions
were worn over long stockings
and were fastened by a garter
with a rosette. Open-sided shoes
with low heels were worn, fastened by a ribbon ties. Across the
body from the right shoulder to
the left hip was worn the broad
baldrick, and in a leather type
frog a sword was carried. The
hair was now quite long and
moustaches and beards were
worn. A tall hat with a wide brim
ornamented with feathers was
worn. The soldier carried a pike.

The young boy, as was usual in
these times, wears the same style
of clothes as his elders. The
doublet, high-waisted and without bombast or padding, was
fastened from neck to waist

with a close row of buttons down the centre. The high neck of the doublet was concealed by the falling band collar. At the waist were ribbon points which attached the trunk hose to the doublet. The short skirt of tabs came to a deep point in front, with the two front tabs coming edge to edge. The upper part of the broad, winged sleeves were paned, and the tight-fitting lower sleeves ended in turned-back lace cuffs. The trunk hose were closely gathered at the waist and fell in folds ending just above the knees. Large rosettes ornamented the trunk hose where they joined the stockings. Large sash garters with rosettes were tied just below the knees. Open-sided shoes with ribbon ties were worn. Similar to the adults the hair was now worn much longer.

27　Lady in black, and Boy, c. 1628

The boy wears a high-waisted doublet with a deep skirt. The doublet was fastened from the neck to the waist by a centre row of buttons. The skirt, made from four tabs, overlapped at the sides, while the two pointed tabs at the front came edge to edge. The breast of the doublet was paned as were the upper winged sleeves and the lower closer-fitting sleeves which ended with a turn-back cuff of lace. The high neck of the doublet was concealed by the falling band collar as were the band strings of the ruff. The 'cloak bag' breeches worn by the boy were gathered at the waist and fell to just below the knees; they were fastened on the outside by ribbon rosettes and sash garters. Openings on the outside of the leg were fastened with buttons, but were allowed to remain open to reveal the linen lining. The open-sided shoes with ribbon rosette ties were still popular. The hair was worn long, with large beret-type hats.

The lady wears the sombre but sumptuous new style of costume. The tight-fitting bodice to the waist was stiff and boned, coming to a slight point in front. It was fastened down the front and a stomacher laced across. A fan-shaped standing band collar encircled the low *décolletage* with lace strips bordering the neckline. The bodice sleeves were ballooned and paned above and below the elbow, and finished with broad splayed turned-back cuffs with vandyked lace borders. The gown was loose, fitting the shoulders and falling in spreading folds to the ground. It was open, fastening at the waist with a ribboned rosette and four narrow sashes across the stomacher, which revealed the under-dress. The large elbow-length sleeves of the gown were slashed and fastened with a large ribboned rosette over the large ballooned bodice sleeves. The hair had a short straight, combed-down fringe with the sides of the hair frizzed or fluffed out around the cheeks to just below the ears. At the back the hair was made up into a flat bun and usually left uncovered.

28 German Soldier Musians, fifer and drummer, c. 1628

The soldier musicians of this period were respected as being non-combatants, and if captured their lives were usually spared. Both the drummers and the fifers had special duties within the army and were not only used for marching but also for signalling, using their instruments to relay messages and commands. The fifer usually carried two or more fifes in his pocket, these being of various size and pitch. The simple six-holed fife, known as a

'zwerch-pfeiff' or Swiss pipe, was first introduced by the mercenary soldiers (mainly Swiss) who served the European rulers. The fife was always associated with the drum; the German name still being 'trommelflote' or drum flute. The side drum of this time was wider and deeper than the drum of today, with the sound much duller, lacking the sharp crisp note of its modern counterpart.

The fifer on the left wears the close-fitting doublet which was long-waisted and stiffened with buckram. The belly pieces, triangular stiffening of pasteboard, were sewn on either side at waist level and each piece placed in a vertical position along the front border. This formed the corset ridge down the 'belly' known as the 'girdlestead', and followed the curve of the waistline. The skirt of tabs overlapped each other; the two front tabs coming deeper in the front and meeting edge to edge. The neckline was V-shaped, and from this emerged a *golillia* or standing band which was worn without a support. The doublet was fastened from neck to waist with a row of close buttons down the centre. The winged sleeves were close-fitting to the wrist and finished with a short turned-back cuff of linen. A narrow waist belt and slings carried the sword. Around the body from the right shoulder to the left hip was a baldrick. The trunk hose were gathered in at the waist, falling into folds and finishing at mid-thigh; being padded they resembled large onion shapes. From mid-thigh to just below the knee were attached the cannions. The ends of the cannions were tied with a ribbon garter and ribbon bows. On the outside seam of the hose was a broad decoration of braid and buttons. The shoes were decorated with large ribbon rosettes. The high-crowned hat was cocked at the front and decorated with a hat band and feathers. The hair was worn long and came to just below the ears.

The drummer wears a sleeveless jerkin which was fairly close-fitting and had deep-squared skirts to hip level. The jerkin was fastened from the rounded neckline to the hem with a centre row of buttons. The close-fitting, slashed sleeves were attached to the wings, and ended in short turned-back cuffs. The full baggy pluderhose were gathered at the waist and fell in folds to the knees, where they finished with ribbon garters and bows on the outside of the leg. The shoes were fastened with ribbon knots. The high-crowned hat, with the wide brim turned down, was decorated with feathers.

29 Velásquez's Spanish Lady, c. 1630

Spanish costume style still adhered to the fashion of the previous century; the farthingale was still being worn in the Spanish and Portuguese courts. The lady, after a painting by Velàsquez, wears the stiff, heavy but beautiful costume of this outmoded fashion. The high-necked bodice was tight-fitting; the standing collar was concealed by the unusual fox fur ruff worn in place of the more formal linen material. The sleeves were close-fitting to the wrists, slightly padded, and had a turned-back cuff of lace. The skirt followed the shape of the understructure of the Spanish farthingale and was gored at the waist making it slope stiffly outwards, giving a smooth flat surface with drapings to the ground. It was heavily decorated with broad guards of gold braid down the centre and around the hem. The close-fitting doublet or waistcoat, which at this period was very fashionable, was similar to that of the male doublet of the earlier period, but without padding and came to a deep rounded point in front. The deep skirt of the doublet flared out from the waist over the hips and curved down to a deep rounded sweep in the front. The neckline of the doublet sloped to a V-shape in the front, and was fastened down the front by a series of large jewelled buttons. The doublet was without sleeves, but at the shoulders were broad wings also decorated with large jewelled buttons. From these wings hung immense hanging sleeves which were edged in wide guards of gold braid. The doublet was heavily decorated with gold braid. Jewelled necklaces and brooches were worn, and a large handkerchief of lawn trimmed with lace was carried. The hair was frizzed and fluffed over pads and arranged in close curls; the side hair being full to just below the ears.

30 German Officer and Lady in riding habit, c. 1630

This plate depicts the fashion of the military man and the riding habit of the ladies of the middle period of the seventeenth century. It was a time of great change, and the abandonment of padding and stiffness was now very apparent except in Spain.

The lady wears the high-necked pleated bodice with a large, oval, closed ruff of lawn. The sleeves were straight and fairly close-fitting, with wings at the shoulders and long sham hanging sleeves. The bodice sleeves had the fashionable deep lawn cuffs turned back from the wrist with wide vandyked lace borders. The skirt was full and gathered; it fell in folds to the ground and, as in the popular style of the day, was worn without a farthingale. The doublet, now called a jacket, was without padding and was close-fitting to the waist, flaring out slightly with the aid of gussets. The skirt of the jacket finished in a straight edge round the hips. The jacket was fastened down the front by a series of hooks and eyes. The 'cavalier' type hat had a moderately high crown with a wide brim usually cocked and trimmed with a hat band and flowing feather plume. The hat was worn over a coif which was not unlike a child's close-fitting bonnet.

The straight riding stick was carried.

The military gentleman wore the high-waisted, deep-skirted leather jerkin. The jerkin had a narrow, flat, turned-down collar and fastened down the centre with a close row of buttons from neck to hem-line. It was sleeveless, but attached under the jerkin wings were sleeves of a softer material which were trimmed with buttons and braid.

'Cavalier' type hat

The front seams of the soft sleeves were left open to reveal the chemise sleeves beneath. They finished with turned-back, lace-bordered cuffs of lawn which were usually concealed by leather gauntlet gloves. Worn around the neck and chest was a collar of steel—the military gorget—the last surviving piece of the suit of armour. Over this was a broad laced falling band which spread from shoulder to shoulder. From the right shoulder across the body to the left hip was slung the broad leather shoulder belt which supported the sword in an ornate leather frog. Around the waist was encircled a broad silk baldrick tied with a large bow at the side. The breeches were the full oval type, often called 'cloak bag' breeches, and fastened below the knees. Also worn were high boot hose with lace tops which were folded over high turned-down soft leather boots which had large spur leathers. A broad-brimmed 'cavalier' hat was worn, similar to that worn by the lady, but was usually uncocked and decorated with larger feather plumes.

31 Lady and Gentleman going to a wedding, c. 1630

By the 1630s the fashions no longer resembled those of the previous decade. The fashionable silhouette of both the male and female had changed. Gone was the massive padding and bombast, in its place new styles with soft folds, draperies, and a profusion of ribbons and lace.

The lady is wearing a basqued

bodice, which was tabbed, similar to the doublet of the male dress. The tabs, deep and square, were laced across the mid-line. The centre tab of the stomacher came to a deep, rounded point in the front, and was plain and unbusked, fastening down the front. The *décolletage* was cut low and round in front, but was higher at the back. It was surrounded by a collar which came from either side spreading out fanwise around the back of the head. A narrow ribbon sash encircled the waistline and finished in a large bow in front. The sleeves of the bodice were ballooned and paned, both above and below the elbows. They were distended by a horsehair stuffing. At the wrists the sleeves were gathered in by draw-strings and ended in large hand ruffs. The fitted bodice gown was joined to a full gathered skirt, and was open down the front. The neckline fitted low on the shoulders. The outer sleeves were tied at the elbow by a ribbon rosette caught in between the stuffed sleeves of the bodice, giving a double balloon effect. The hair style was a short fringe with the side hair fluffed out and frizzed from side

Falling band collar, 1630

partings. The back hair was coiled into a bun just below the crown of the head and usually left uncovered. A folding fan was carried.

The gentleman depicts the advent of the cavalier fashion; the jerkin or waistcoat replacing the doublet. The jerkin was slightly fitted to the waist, then flared out gently over the hips and ended just below in a straight line. The jerkin was fastened from the neck to the hem-line with brandenburgs—horizontal strips of braid, or loops with buttons. The sleeves were open at the seam revealing the full sleeves of the chemise or shirt. Brandenburgs also decorated the sleeves on either side of the seam. The shirt sleeves finished with hand falls or wrist cuffs with smaller wrist ruffles both laced and vandyked. Ribbon rosettes encircled the waistline. The neckline of the jerkin was hidden by the large falling band which sloped down and spread from shoulder to shoulder and was tied with band strings which were allowed to hang down. The falling band matched the hand falls, being lace bordered and vandyked. The moderately full, long-legged breeches, called Spanish hose, fell to just below the knees and fastened with ribbon loops. The breeches were decorated down the outside seams and halfway down the front with brandenburgs. Short leather boots with cup-shaped falling tops of soft leather were ornamented with 'butterfly' spur leathers. The large 'cavalier' type hat, slightly cocked on one side, was trimmed with a hat band and feathers. The hair during this period was usually full and curly, covering the ears. A moustache and vandyke beard were sometimes worn. An ebony stick was often carried.

32 Lady and Gentleman in Court dress, c. 1630

The lady is wearing a tight-fitting bodice with a stomacher coming to a deep point in the front. The stomacher was stiffened and boned and fastened down the front by a row of close set buttons. The bodice had a low *décolletage* edged with lace strips. A spreading fan collar surrounded the neck. The sleeves of the bodice were large, balloon-shaped, and paned above and below the elbow. Above the wrists the sleeves were pulled in by a running draw-string, then finished off with a turned-back cuff. The skirt was loosely gathered at the waist then fell in irregular folds to the ground. The gown had a fitted bodice joined to a full gathered skirt and was open down the front. The neckline was low on the shoulders. The straight sleeves, which were open down the front seam, were tied by a ribbon bow at the bend of the elbow. These sleeves were hardly visible at the front when worn with the balloon bodice sleeves. Around the waist was worn a narrow ribbon cord. The hair, which hung down below the ears, was brushed straight back from the forehead and temples, and fluffed out at the sides. Pearl necklaces, brooches and jewellery were still popular, although the lavish use of these was becoming unfashionable. Large feather fans with highly decorative handles were, however, very fashionable.

For the male, the doublet was now high-waisted, not quite so close-fitting, and was almost without stiffening. The tabs, or skirts, were more imposing than previously. The two front tabs were deeply pointed in front, meeting edge to edge. The doublet now resembled more of a jacket, and was buttoned down the centre from the neck to the waist with a close row of buttons. Surrounding the stiff high neck was a stand-fall ruff which completely concealed the neck line. The doublet was paned at the chest front and back, revealing the full linen or silk shirt beneath. Ribbon loops ornamented and encircled the waistline. The winged sleeves were wide and paned to the elbow, then close-fitting to the wrists. Decorative gauntlet gloves concealed the turned-back lace cuffs. Long-legged breeches were full to the knee, where they were fringed with ribbon loops. The soft leather boots, which had by now become very fashionable for both outdoor and indoor use, had their tops turned down to reveal the silk stockings. Large spur leathers were worn, some-

times without metal spurs, and used as decoration only. The hair was worn long; it fell to the shoulders from a centre parting. The moustache and vandyke beard were still very popular. Canes were often carried.

33 Cavalier Officer and Lady, c. 1630

The French fashions were now being quickly adopted by most European courts; farthingales and ruffs finally disappearing.

The French style, with the bodice cut low on the shoulders and the low, square *décolletage*, was now the accepted mode for the lady. The *décolletage* was trimmed with a lace collar and cut in the vandyke style. The bodice was high-waisted. The sleeves were short and very full to just above the elbows, then drawn in loosely to allow the full frill of the chemise to emerge at elbow length. The closed full skirt was gathered at the waist, then allowed to fall naturally in folds to the ground. The French style of hairdressing was worn. The hair at the back was coiled into a flat bun, and the sides dressed in short curls around the ears; one or two of the curls were sometimes left to hang freely down to the shoulders. Combed down across the forehead were short curls which formed a fringe. The hair was decorated with jewels.

The cavalier gentleman wears a sleeveless buff coat (buff being an ox-hide treated with oil) often called a leather jerkin. This coat worn by most military men was fairly close-fitting, high-waisted and had a deep skirt reaching down to just below hip length. The skirt overlapped in front, and had a slit at the back. The rounded neckline was without a collar, this being concealed by a falling band type collar which lay from shoulder to shoulder. This collar was made of point lace and was cut in the vandyke style. The coat fastened from the neck to the waist by a close row of buttons and loops down the front. A sleeve of soft material was sewn on under the narrow welt wing, and the front seam of this sleeve was left open to the wrist to reveal the fine, full shirt sleeve beneath. The sleeves ended with a point lace similar to the collar. The loose breeches reached to the knees and were tied with ribbon garters. The boot-hose had lace tops which showed above the high soft leather boots. The spur 'butterfly' leathers were both useful and decorative. Encircling the waist was a wide silk baldrick sash tied in a huge bow on the left hip. The sword was carried from a waist belt and frog. The 'cavalier' style hat had a moderately high crown, a very broad brim and was usually worn in a cocked position. The hair was long and in the English style; the ringlets not reaching lower than the back of the collar. A moustache and a neat pointed beard continued to be in fashion.

34 The wearing of the cloak, c. 1630

The French cloak, or *manteau à la reitre*, was the most popular style of cloak and lasted for almost one hundred years in one form or another. It was worn sometimes without a collar, but could also be worn with a flat rectangular 'sailor collar' at the back. In length the cloak reached the knees, but was sometimes worn a little longer. It could be worn draped around the body without any form of fastening.

Top left Rear view of the cape worn over one shoulder and gathered up over the arm.

Top right The cloak worn at an angle with the cords of the collar over the left shoulder and under the right shoulder.

Bottom left The cloak hanging on the left shoulder with the cords of the collar over one shoulder only, then gathered up under the right arm.

Bottom right Front view of the cloak gathered up over the left arm. For all formal dress the ruff or falling band collars were worn outside the cloak.

35 Musketeer and country Girl in pattens, c. 1633

The country's woman's clothes, although not so attractive as those of the wealthier city dwellers, were nonetheless an attempt to keep up with the fashionable trend of the day. The bodice was close-fitting and high-waisted with a basque. The basque was tabbed in the same way as the male doublet, being both deep and square and sewn together. The bodice was open in front and pulled together by means of lacing. A stomacher was pinned to the front. The neckline formed a low *décolletage* in front but was cut higher at the back. A plain neckerchief—a large square of fine material folded diagonally—was worn over the shoulders like a shawl and fastened in the front at the throat. The full skirt was gathered at the waist and fell in folds to the ground. It was often hitched up in front and at the sides, revealing the under-skirt or petticoat. The materials used were much coarser than those of the wealthier classes. A coif or day cap, usually of a white material, sometimes edged with a narrow band of lace, was worn over the hair and round the back of the neck and was formed to fit over the bun at the back of the head. Pattens were worn; these were wooden-soled overshoes raised up on iron rings. They were secured by straps and worn with ordinary shoes. They were ideal for their purpose, which was to keep the shoes and the hems of skirts free from the mud and filth of the highways, caused by the unhygienic conditions of this period. These metal 'stilt' overshoes were worn, in various styles, by all classes both in the towns and country.

The musketeer wears the hip-length buff jerkin as did many of the military men of the day. The jerkin was sleeveless and opened down the front to reveal the shirt with the falling collar beneath. Close-fitting sleeves

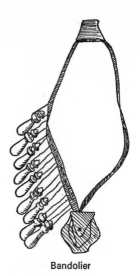

Bandolier

ners' for the matchlock gun, was carried from the left shoulder across the body to the right hip. This musketeer carried a wooden rest which stood about a metre and a half high, with a fork of steel on the top to support the heavy matchlock barrel whilst firing. He also carried a coil of slow-burning 'match' and when required, both ends were lit as a precaution against one going out. A high-crowned hat with a wide brim decorated with feathers was worn.

36 Nobleman and Boy in hunting attire, c. 1635

Hunting was a very popular pastime at this period especially in the fashion conscious world of Spain.

The nobleman is wearing a leather jerkin which was close-fitting to the body, had a high waistline and a deep skirt over-lapping in front; there was also a slit at the back. The jerkin was without a collar and came to a small V-shape at the neck. This was filled in by a falling band collar of lawn decorated with a lace border and cut in the vandyke style. The fastening of the jerkin was from the neck to to the waist by close lacing. A

were sewn under the wings on the shoulders; the cuffs of these sleeves were hidden under short gauntlet gloves. The full pluder-hose type breeches were gathered at the waist and fell in irregular folds to just below the knees, where they were tied with ribbon garters and had ribbon knots on the outside of the legs. The outside seams of the trunk hose were decorated with but-tons and loops. Coarse linen stockings, rolled down, were worn to protect the finer stock-ings worn beneath. High shoes were worn with a ribbon tie bow. A bandolier, with flasks, bullet bag, charges, and keys or 'span-

narrow belt encircled the waist. The loose winged sleeves were worn hanging. Close-fitting sleeves of a softer material were attached under the wings. The trunk hose, probably made from either soft leather or material, were in the 'cloak bag' breeches style. These breeches were gathered at the waist and closed just below the knees, fastening on the outside by a ribbon rosette. The breeches were often trimmed with braid down the outside seam of each leg. High boots of soft leather were worn. A tall-crowned hat of soft leather or material was worn and placed in any position to suit the wearer. A broad brim could form a peaked hat. The plain, long gauntlet gloves worn were of soft leather extending well above the wrists.

The little boy, as was usual, dressed in similar clothes to the adults. The leather jerkin was loose-fitting, rather like a smock, possibly fastening at the side or back. There was no collar but the neckline opened in a small V-shape and was filled by a falling band collar of lawn, usually lace decorated. Attached to the wings were the tubular hanging sleeves of leather and softer material

sleeves, close-fitting to the wrists. The full oval breeches were fastened just below the knees with a ribbon rosette. Long soft leather boots were worn. A soft leather or material low-crowned hat with a peak was worn at a slight angle. Plain gauntlet gloves of soft leather were worn. The hair styles remained long, falling below the ears. The young boy wore a fringe.

37 English Earl and Lady in Court dress, c. 1635

The new English styles followed very closely those of the Louis XIII period of fashion in France. The bodice of the new styles for women was high-waisted, worn with a basque. The basque was similar to that of the male doublet with the tabs, or skirts, being deep and square and the centre tab coming to a round point from the stomacher. The bodice had a low *décolletage* with a broad lace-edged bertha—a wide lingerie collar which came from the edges of the *décolletage* over the shoulders and around the back. A narrow ribbon sash followed the waistline and tied in a spreading bow. The sleeves were full to the elbow with close pleats at the shoulders and at the elbows. At the elbows they were gathered on to a band, or sometimes drawn with a running string, but left loose enough to allow the frilled undersleeve to come through. The closed skirt was loosely gathered at the waist and fell to the ground in folds. It was often slightly trained. The hair style had a wispy fringe across the forehead with the side hair cut short and hanging in ringlets over the ears. The hair at the back was drawn up into a bun.

The man, following the fashionable trend, wears the embroidered, close-fitting doublet which was high-waisted and had deep-skirted tabs. The centre tabs came to a deep point in the front and met edge to edge. The doublet had a standing collar which was concealed by a falling band collar of lawn and lace vandykes. The fastening was from neck to waist by a centre row of buttons. The wings were now quite small with fairly loose sleeves hanging to the wrists. The sleeves had a longitudinal slash on the front seam which revealed the full lawn chemise sleeve below. The slash was edged with buttons and loops. The sleeve finished with a turned-back lace cuff which matched the falling band. The long-legged breeches were shaped to the hips and thighs and ended just below the knees, where they were closed with ribbon sashes and large bows on the outside of the leg. Down the outside seam of the breeches were decorations of loops of braid and buttons. Silk stockings were worn with open-sided, low-heeled shoes which were tied with shoe roses. A large cloak was draped around the figure. A sword hung from a narrow waist belt with slings. The hair was worn long and a moustache and vandyke beard were worn.

38 Ladies' hair and head-dress fashions, c. 1610–60

Top left The Dutch style of coiffure of *c.* 1632. The hair was combed down in the front to give a thin fringe on the forehead; the remainder was brushed straight back and coiled into a flat bun at the back. Sometimes this bun was decorated. The side hair was parted and frizzed out, hanging to the neck.

Top right The English fashion during the 1640s. A tall-crowned hat with a wide brim and a lawn lace-bordered under-cap hiding most of the lady's coiffure.

Centre left The French 'cornet' style of the 1630s. The cornet was a coif-type cap which fitted the back of the head and curled down either side to cover the ears. The centre piece was deep and pointed. A stiffened back piece standing upright decorated the cap.

Centre A Dutch style of 1610. A tall-crowned hat cocked high on the left was decorated with a hat band and jewels. The hair was partially covered with a lace under-cap.

Centre right The German 'cornet' style of 1630. A cap of linen which had a lace border and a gauze front wired and shaped around the face.

Bottom left The English style of 1616. The hair was brushed back from the forehead and temples with pieces of hair combed down just in front of the ears. A wide-brimmed, tall-crowned hat of beaver with a decorated hat band was worn.

Bottom right The Dutch style of 1660. The hair was brushed away from the forehead and wired corkscrew curls massed on either side of the face. The hair at the back was twisted into a flat bun.

39 Countess and Child, c. 1640

The fashions of the English court remained under French influence. The lady is wearing a high-waisted bodice which was close-fitting and stiffened with whalebone. The *décolletage* was cut low in the front and high at the back. It encircled the bust and partially bared the shoulders. The lace of the chemise bordered the *décolletage*. The fastening of the bodice was at the back. The sleeves, following the contour of the bodice, were full with a wide lace-edged opening just above the elbow. The just below elbow-length sleeves of the chemise with their frilly ends emerged below the bodice sleeve. The full skirt was gathered at the waist and hung in loose folds to the ground. A narrow jewelled belt encircled the waistline. The hair style, rumoured to have been introduced from Austria, had a short fringe of curls across the forehead. The hair was then combed back to form a knot or bun at the back of the head. This was sometimes covered with a small caul. The side hair was longer and now hung in corkscrew ringlets down to the shoulders. The hair was decorated with ribbon bows. Ear-rings of pearl clusters were worn.

The little girl was dressed in a similar style. The bodice was high-waisted and close-fitting, being stiffened with whalebone. The square *décolletage* was cut low in the front and high at the back. The sleeves were full, tapering down to just above the wrists and ended with a deep turned-back cuff of lace which was vandyked. The skirt was gathered at the waist and allowed to fall in vertical folds to the ground. The hair was in the same style as that of the lady, and decorated with ribbon. Jewellery was worn by children in much the same way as adults.

40 Merchants' Wives, English and Dutch fashions, c. 1640

These English and Dutch styles still retained much of the previous fashions. The English lady on the left wore the close-fitting bodice which was high waisted with a low *décolletage* and a chemisette fill-in. The neck was encircled with a large ruff, oval in shape, which was very fashionable for married ladies when worn with the low *décolletage*. The sleeves were full and puffed to the wrist, in the 'bishop' style, and finished with a deep turn-back cuff with a lace edge.

The 'sugarloaf' hat had a high crown which sloped to a narrow flat top. The brim was broad and flat, dipping slightly in front and at the back. A simple narrow hat band was the only decoration. The hat was worn over a white coif or under-cap. This type of hat was usually worn by married ladies of the middle classes, and by country women during the 1640s. The hair was sometimes arranged over the ear-flaps of the coif. A medium-sized fur muff was carried by the more wealthy merchants' wives.

The Dutch fashion for middle-class ladies favoured the basqued bodice. The bodice was short-waisted, the tabs of the basque being deep and squared. The short sleeves of the bodice were castellated and just covered the shoulder joins. The bodice was paned and fastened down the centre of the front. The undersleeves were close-fitting and long to the wrist, ending in a turn-back cuff which was edged with lace and vandyked. Around the high neckline of the bodice was a closed cart-wheel ruff worn mainly by married women. This type of ruff was more popular in Holland than in any other European country. The closed skirt was gathered loosely at the waist, falling in irregular folds to the ground. A plain white apron was worn both in the home and as an attractive accessory for the skirt. A wired day-cap was worn which was placed over the back of the head and around the back of the neck. It was shaped to fit over the popular 'bun and coil' of the hair at the back. The cap was not tied under the chin, but was attached to the hair by a pinner.

41 Lady in 'chaperone' and mask, with Nobleman, c. 1640

The lady is wearing an informal out-of-doors costume. On her head she wore the 'chaperone', a soft hood which covered the head and framed the face. This was secured under the chin by a small bow of ribbon ties. This head covering could be worn either by itself or over an under-cap of lace or a coif. Over her dress she wore the long, voluminous 'cassock' or overcoat. This was an adaptation from the coat worn by the military foot- and horse-soldiers, and often described as the 'horseman's coat'. Some had a large cap attachment reaching to hip level. Around the neckline was a small, round, turned-down collar, and the coat was fastened from the neck to the hem with buttons down the centre of the front. A shortened version of this costume was worn by country people. On her face the lady wore a half-mask ending just below the nose; this was secured by ribbon ties round the back of the head. Masks were very popular and were mainly worn by ladies. They could be worn for a variety of reasons such as attending the theatre or even as a disguise for out of doors. They came in various shapes and sizes; some were oval and made to cover the whole face, and were held in position by a button gripped between the teeth. They were made in velvet, satin, taffeta or silk, were lined with thin skins or silk, and came in a variety of colours. A large feather fan with a decorative handle and a mirror was carried on a ribbon cord attached to a waist girdle. A fairly large fur muff was carried either in the hand or on a cord from around the neck.

'Chaperone' hood

The man wears the close-fitting, high-waisted doublet, which came to a blunt point in front. Deep skirts flared out to mid-thigh, overlapping slightly in the front. The breast front and the back had vertical panes down to waist level and revealed the coloured lining beneath. From the small projecting wings hung the sleeves which were full and paned from the shoulder to the elbow, then close-fitting to the wrist. The panes showed the lining beneath. The wrist cuffs were hidden by the high gauntlet gloves of leather. The neck was encircled by a broad falling band of vandyke-edged lace. The long-legged breeches, or Spanish hose, were worn. These were full at the hips, then narrowed down the leg ending below the knees. High boots of fine leather were worn, and these were topped with the fine lace turn-down of the boot hose. The spur leathers were the large 'butterfly' type. These leathers were originally broad bands across the ankle, but became so large by the 1640s that they spread over the whole foot. The hair was worn long and the popular moustache and van-dyke beard were still worn. The large 'cavalier' style hat with decorative feathers completed the costume. No fashionable gentleman was without his sword, which he carried on his left side.

42 Country Gentleman and his Wife, c. 1640

The lady is dressed in the 'new style' which started in the late 1620s and lasted until the 1650s. She wore the high-waisted, basqued bodice. The basque, like the male doublet, was tabbed; the tabs being squared and deep. The tab in the centre of the front came slightly lower to a rounded point, and belonged to the stomacher. The plain stomacher was pinned to the front borders. The neckline formed a low *décolletage* in front but was cut higher at the back in a square shape. The broad bertha of deeply bordered lace was worn with a large, square, lace-edged neckerchief. This, when folded diagonally, was placed over the shoulders and fastened at the neck by a small brooch. The 'coat' sleeve was double; the upper sleeve finishing at the elbow, the lower sleeve close-fitting and ending at the wrist with a lace turned-back cuff. The skirt was gathered loosely at the waist, and fell in irregular vertical folds to the ground. Around the waist was a ribboned girdle from which was suspended a pomander. Ear-rings were worn, but the lavish use of jewellery was becoming unfashionable.

The gentleman wears the ornamental leather jerkin or buff coat. This was of military origin and became very popular for fashionable civilian wear. The coat was close-fitting with a high waistline and a deep skirt reaching hip length; it was slit at the back, and quite often at the sides. It was without a collar but was sometimes worn open down the front to mid-chest and turned back to give a narrow lapel effect. From the wings, hanging towards the back, were loose tubular pieces worn as decorative hanging sleeves. Also hanging from the coat wings were close-fitting

sleeves, usually of a soft cloth material, often trimmed with lace or braid in longitudinal stripes. This cloth sleeve was sewn on under the wings, and finished in a deep turned-back lace cuff; the effect given was of an underlying doublet. The neckline of the coat was concealed under a broad lace falling-band collar. The coat was decorated overall in stripes of braid and buttons. The full breeches, or Spanish hose as they were known, stretched from the waist to below the knee. Although somewhat full they were shaped to the figure, narrowing down to end just below the knee. Here they were tied with ribbon garters forming large bows on the outside of the leg, from which hung lace pieces. The breeches, like the jerkin, were decorated with braid and lace. The round-toed shoes were surmounted by large shoe roses. The hair was cut moderately short and a moustache and vandyke beard were worn.

43 Children of a Royal Family, c. 1641

The children of royalty and well-to-do parents were dressed in the most lavish styles and fashions made from sumptuous materials.

The young girl is dressed in the style of the fashionable ladies of the court. The bodice was short-waisted and was fastened at the front, either by lacing or clasps. In front it was shaped into a V-form, showing a laced chemisette fill-in, giving the effect of a stomacher being present. The bodice had a low square *décolletage* in front with a higher cut square back. A deep, lace-bordered collar, a broad bertha, surrounded the *décolletage* and ended just in front of the shoulders Across the front it bordered the neckline as a narrow strip. The coat sleeve was double; the over-sleeve ending at the elbow, the sleeve beneath coming lower and ending in a turned-back lace cuff. The skirt was gathered at the waist and fell in folds to the ground. The inverted V-shape opening in the front showed the underskirt, usually of the same colour and material as the dress and skirt. A narrow ribbon girdle followed the contours of the waistline and was tied into a spreading bow on the side. The hair was brushed straight back from the forehead, with just the wisp of a fringe or just the odd curl or two hanging down; the side hair hung full and loose to the shoulders. Jewels ornamented the bun formed at the back of the head. Apart from a necklace and jewelled ribbon knots on the dress, lavish jewellery remained unfashionable.

The boy is dressed in the same style as the fashionable gentleman of the court. He wore the high-waisted, loose-fitting doublet. There was no padding and just the minimum of stiffening. The neckline had a short standing collar. The doublet was fastened from neck to waist by a row of close buttons, but more often than not remained unbuttoned from chest to waist to reveal the elegant chemise shirt beneath. It was paned down the breast and at the back, matching the sleeve fashion. Down to the elbow the sleeve was full and paned, then close-fitting to the wrist ending in a deep turned-back cuff of van-dyked lace. The neck was encircled with a broad lace falling band. The long-legged breeches, pleated into a waist band, were shaped to the body and fell to just below the knees, where they were closed by a ribbon sash garter with large bows on the outside of the leg. Silk stockings were worn. The shoes, with side openings, had large ribbon bows as fastenings. Narrow ornamental leather slings were worn to support the small hanger sword. A wide-brimmed hat with a moderately high conical crown and a decorative hat band was fashionable. The French type of cloak was worn draped over the body. The hair was worn long, falling to the shoulders from a central parting.

44 Ladies in summer fashions, c. 1643

The lady on the left is wearing a spring or early summer fashion. The high-waisted bodice was made with a basque. The basque tabs were sewn together to form a deep downward point in front. The bodice was fastened at the back by a series of clasps; it was worn without a stomacher but had a chemisette fill-in which was laced across. The neck had a low *décolletage* in front but was cut much higher at the back. The neck was encircled with a bertha type collar which enclosed the shoulders of the bodice, and ended at the edge of the shoulders. The bodice had a turned-down narrow lace edging in front. Over this was a lace-edged square neckerchief which

was folded corner-wise and fastened at the base of the throat. The sleeves were in two parts; an oversleeve or 'coat' sleeve which reached the elbows like an enlarged drooping epaulette, and an undersleeve which came a little lower than elbow length and ended with a turned-back cuff finished with lace. The moderately full skirt was gathered in at the waist and fell in folds to the ground. It could be open or closed. The hair was brushed straight back with two side partings, then curled into corkscrew curls cascading to the shoulders. The back hair was caught up into a flat-topped bun which was often concealed by a caul.

The lady on the right is dressed in a high summer fashion of the period. The bodice followed the trend of fashion and was high waisted with a basque.

Head decoration, 1643

The neckline of the low *dé-colletage* was encircled by a broad bertha, deeply edged with lace, and coming well off the shoulders. The sleeves consisted of an epaulette, an oversleeve, and an undersleeve. The oversleeve was puffed and paned; the undersleeve, which came only to the elbow, was edged with lace. Long elbow-length gloves, usually plain but sometimes embroidered, were close-fitting and always worn with short-sleeved bodices. The full skirt, which was gathered in at the waist, was frequently bunched up in a casual way to show the full elegance and beautiful material of the underskirt. The hair followed the mode of the day with shoulder length curls and a bun covered by a caul. Over the head and face was a plain gauze veil which draped over the shoulders and hung down in front. A folding fan was carried.

45 English Lady in furs and mask, and a Dutch Lady, c. 1643

The English lady on the left, although clad for winter, wears an extremely elegant costume. The fashionable high-waisted bodice with the low *décolletage*

was still worn despite inclement weather. The low *décolletage* was undoubtably covered by both a broad bertha collar and a neckerchief. The sleeves were reasonably close-fitting, ending just above the wrists with a turned-back cuff, often open behind. A lace turned-back cuff was added. The skirt was moderately full and rather heavy. It was gathered in at the waist and allowed to fall to the ground in irregular vertical folds. Both the skirt and the underskirt were sometimes bunched up in a variety of ways, exposing the more delicate silken fabric of the under-petticoat. The hair style, in the fashionable mode of the caul covering the flat bun at the back, was completely covered with a hood. The hood, or 'chaperone', was of a soft material, often silken lined and worn only for outdoors. It was tied under the chin with a small ribbon bow, and was often wired to curve around the face. A deep fur stole was worn around the neck and shoulders, and a matching large fur muff was carried in the hand. On the face is shown a half-mask of black velvet covering the upper part of the face only. It was secured by ties around the back of the head.

The small Venetian half-face mask, or *loup* (wolf) mask, was the most popular, and was normally made of black velvet and lined in white silk. The mask was worn to protect the complexion. Even at home a night mask was worn to protect the skin. Later, in the eighteenth century, the small mask was worn in the Americas by women and children. Shoes were similar to those of the male fashion, and even had the large, ribbon shoe rosettes.

The lady on the right wears the typical Dutch fashion of that period. The high-waisted bodice had a deep V-shaped stomacher. The old style of the padded front still continued in Dutch costume, being effected by the curve of the deep stomacher. The neckline trimming was the popular fashion of the closed cartwheel ruff which tilted up at the back and down in the front. The heavy full skirt was gathered into the waist and fell in folds to the ground. It was hitched up to about knee level and revealed the underskirt which also reached the ground. The close-fitting sleeves came to just below elbow length and ended with deep turned-back lace cuffs. A cap of

linen, edged with lacverede, co the hair and framed the face. Long elbow length gloves were often worn.

46 Petticoat and loose breeches fashion, mid-seventeenth century

Top left The short doublet with a little stiffening but without padding. The skirt was short and tabbed. Under the skirt hung multiple ribbon loops called 'fancies'. The neck had a round standing collar, usually stiffened with buckram. The doublet was fastened down the centre of the front with a row of buttons from neck to waist. The full sleeves had narrow panes to the wrists and were also trimmed with ribbon fancies. The petticoat

Petticoat breeches

breeches, often called 'rhine-graves', were almost skirt-like in appearance. They had very wide legs pleated onto a waistband and fell to the knees. Bunches of ribbon loops were worn on the outside edges at knee level.

Top right A glove worn about the second half of the seventeenth century. It was embroidered and trimmed with ribbon work.

Centre right The hat of a small boy from about 1650. The crown was fairly tall, tapering slightly to a flat top. The wide brim was cocked on either side and the hat band ended in a ribbon bow in front.

Bottom left A high-tongued leather shoe, fastened with a buckle and strap and decorated with ribbon knots at the toe.

Bottom right A boy's costume with the same fashionable characteristics as those of the adults. The doublet was high-waisted with a short tabbed skirt with eyelet holes used for decorative purposes, as at this period (1650) the breeches were fastened under a short skirt. The doublet had a high-standing collar and was fastened down the centre of the front from neck to waist by buttons and loops. The sleeves

joined the armhole without a wing, and were full to the wrists ending in turned-back cuffs. The front seam was slit from shoulder to wrist cuff to reveal a chemise shirt beneath. The open breeches, which were like very wide shorts, fell to just below the knee. The outside seam was decorated at the bottom of the breeches with a bunch of ribbon fancies. From the waistband to the fork, the breeches were closed by 'fly buttons'.

47 Autumnal fashions of a Lady and Child, c. 1650

The little girl is dressed in the height of early autumnal fashion of *c.* 1649–50. The bodice was short waisted, with the neck forming a low *décolletage* in front, coming higher at the back, although a little lower than previously. The *décolletage* was cut in the off-the-shoulder style, and was encircled by a bertha collar, deeply bordered with lace and ending just in front of the shoulders. The sleeve was full and ended just below the elbow, where it was gathered by drawstring and finished with a deep cuff with a broad lace border. The front seam was open revealing the brocaded lining beneath;

this was probably joined to the oversleeve. The full skirt was gathered at the waist and fell in folds to the ground. Over the bodice and the front of the skirt was worn an apron with a bib. The girl's hair followed the fashionable coiffure of the day. The hair was brushed straight back from the forehead with two side partings at the temples; the hair then being formed into corkscrew curls falling to the shoulders. The back hair was brushed up to a tight flat bun which was usually covered by a caul. A laced day-cap was worn and arranged to frame the face.

The lady is wearing an autumn fashion, as depicted by Wenceslaus Hollar. The bodice was tight-fitting to the waist, coming to a slight point in front. It was stiff and boned, and fastened down the front by small buttons. The *décolletage* was low and cut horizontally, surrounding the bosom and coming off the shoulder. It was draped by a broad lace bertha and edged in the front by a frill of lace. A large square neckerchief, with a broad border of lace, was worn over the shoulders and *décolletage*, and fastened at the throat by a brooch. A full sleeve fell to the

elbow and finished in a deep turned-back cuff of lace. Close-fitting elbow-length gloves, were worn. The moderately full skirt was gathered in at the waist, often slightly trained, and fell in folds to the ground. Over the front of the skirt was an elegant white linen apron with a lace border. Over the head was a soft hood or 'chaperone'; this covered the fashionable hair style and day-cap. The hood, which framed the face, was fastened under the chin, usually with a ribbon bow. A shawl or scarf, sometimes matching the 'chaperone', was worn around the shoulders and fastened in front on the bodice.

48 A young Spanish Princess, c. 1659

At this time the Spanish still continued to follow their own dictates of fashion. The young lady wears the same basic costume that had been fashionable for almost fifty years. The close-fitting bodice, moderately long-fronted, was joined to the stiff basque of the Spanish farthingale, which tilted down in the front and up at the back. The low, round neckline, horizontal and boat shaped, was encircled with a deep bertha collar. This low *décolletage* exposed the shoulders and the back, but came high over the bust. Accentuation of the bosom was not a part of Spanish fashion and often sheets of metal were inserted in the bodice to retard the development of young girls' breasts. In the centre of the front of the bertha was a large ribboned rosette, fastened on with a jewelled brooch. The sleeves were full to the elbow, then gathered onto a band which was loose enough to permit the full frilled sleeve of the chemise to come through, and end at the wrist with a turned-back lace cuff. The sleeves were paned, revealing the sleeves of the chemise. The farthingale structure, concealed by the stiff basque, was now made of oval-shaped hoops, being flattish in the front and back, but very wide at the sides. It expanded abruptly out from the waist and continued down to the ground, the bottom hoop being as wide as the height of the person wearing the costume. The skirt fitted over the structure and fell to the ground in rather stiff folds. The whole silhouette was square-shaped. The hair style always followed the silhouette of the dress itself. The hair was flat on

Spanish coiffure

the top, being brushed off the face and plaited, puffed and curled. It was tied and fastened with ribbons, hairpins and ornamental pieces. It hung to the shoulders standing away from the head in a very unnatural coiffure. It was also decorated with hanging plumes.

49 Dutch Nobleman and his Wife, c. 1660

The 1660s brought back into fashion the tight lacing of the earlier period of modes. The lady wore the close-fitting busked and boned bodice. The bodice was like those of the previous fashions, long waisted and dipping to a deep point in front. The *décolletage* was cut low, horizontally surrounding the bust and sloping off the shoulders; the neckline was edged with the lace of the chemise. The deep broad lace bertha was boat-shaped and encircled the *décolletage*. The sleeve was full and moderately balloon-shaped. It ended at the elbow where it was caught onto a band which was loose enough to allow the full frilled sleeve of the chemise to come through. The full skirt was gathered into small pleats at the waist, then allowed to fall to the ground in vertical folds. It was often slightly trained. The front was open to reveal the underskirt or petticoat, usually of a contrasting material, sometimes a little shorter than the overskirt. The fashionable coiffure continued as in the previous decade, with the slight variation that the corkscrew curls were massed on either side and then wired out from the face. Ribbon knots were popular both as hair ornamentation and wrist and dress accessories. Lavish jewellery was not a popular fashion.

The gentleman of fashion continued to wear the short unstiffened doublet. Its skirts were merely a narrow tabbed edging under which were trimmings of ribbon loops. The high-standing neck was stiffened with buckram. The fastening was from neck to waist with a row of buttons down the centre front. These were usually fastened down to the chest only, the rest left open to reveal the protruding shirt between the skimpy doublet and the breeches. The sleeves were full with the front seam slit to reveal the full upper part of the shirt sleeve, and finished just below the elbow, where they were fastened. Below the fastening the lower half of the shirt sleeve came to the wrist and ended with a full wrist frill. The high stiff neck-band was concealed by a falling band which was deep and shaped like a bib; the two front edges meeting edge to edge. The collar was square-ended and spread from shoulder to shoulder; broad lace borders were very fashionable. The knee-length open breeches, or petticoat breeches, like very wide shorts, were worn. These were decorated with ribbon loops on the lower part of the outside seam. The wearing of two pairs of stockings was considered very fashionable. Stirrup hose had large tops which were turned down and spread out below the knee; these tops or frills were called port canons. The hair was worn long, moustaches were now slightly drooping and beards merely a tuft under the lower lip.

50 Dutch Gentleman in petticoat breeches with Lady, c. 1665

This fashionable Dutch gentleman of *c.* 1665 wearing the petticoat breeches costume shows this extreme fashion at its best. He wore the short skimpy doublet which did not even reach the waistline. It had a stiff standing collar and buttoned down the centre front with a row of close buttons. It was never fastened lower than the chest, because from there on the shirt protruded in the space between the sparse doublet and the breeches. The neck was encircled by a falling band which stretched from shoulder to shoulder, like a large bib. The falling lawn band, often seen with an inverted box-pleat, had rounded corners and was decorated with a deep lace border. The sleeves, with the front seam slit, finished just below the elbows. Through the slit and below the fastening was revealed the full sleeve of the shirt with the large frilled falling cuff. The petticoat breeches known as pantaloons, or 'rhine-graves', had very large wide legs pleated on to a waist band, then falling to the knee in heavy vertical folds. They were fastened by a button at the waist-line above the front centre opening. In appearance they looked like a full, knee-length, divided skirt. They were profusely decorated around the waist and down the lower part of the outside seam with fringes of large ribbon loops; the hem was bound with ribbon. Stockings were worn, and over these a pair of stirrup hose which had a large decorative top, as much as two metres wide, which when turned down over a garter just below the knee became large cone-shaped frills. These were called canons or port canons. Shoes were square-toed, open-sided and had high square

Deep falling band collar

heels. The tongue was square and rose high over the ankle. The shoes were fastened by drooping ribbon bunches. The full cloak, without sleeves, was worn over both shoulders. The hair hung to the shoulders. The tall 'sugar-loaf' hat was the most popular, the crown being conical in shape, narrowing to a flat top. The brim was broad and usually trimmed with ribbon loops or feathers.

This Dutch lady of fashion wears a silk or satin costume with the close-fitting, boned and long-waisted bodice coming to a deep point in front. The *décolletage* was low cut and encircled by a large velvet collar, high at the back covering the shoulders, and fastened in the front. The front and back of the bodice were decorated with velvet strips. The full, baggy sleeves were drawn in at the elbows from which emerged the full sleeves of the chemise with frill. The sleeves were attached to the sloping shoulders of the bodice. The full skirt was closely gathered into small pleats at the waist and fell in irregular folds to the ground; the skirt was slightly trained. The hair was brushed back from the forehead, leaving hanging side pieces. At the back

it was caught up in a round coil plait.

51 Fashionable Lady in evening dress, c. 1668

The female costume of this period was quite simple in contrast to the excessively decorated and extreme fashions of the males with their absurd petticoat breeches costume. The feminine gown had a close-fitting, boned bodice which, because of the long waist, dipped to a deep point in front, creating a slimmer look. The bodice was worn with a close-fitting corset which was high under the arms and over the bosom; both corset and bodice were laced at the back. The neckline was low cut in a rounded shape which encircled the *décolletage* and bared the shoulders. The *décolletage* was edged by the lace of the chemisette. The sleeves were full to the elbow, and left open to reveal the full frilled sleeves of the chemisette. The full skirt was gathered in pleats at the waist and hung in folds to the ground. It was usually open in front and caught up over an underskirt or petticoat. A train was present, both on the overskirt and on the underskirt; this being very fashionable at the time. Shawls or scarves were very common and were often worn with a low *décolletage*. The hair style was called a *coiffure à la ninon*. The sides were cut fairly short or pushed back off the face, with curls, called *confidants*, bunched on each side, then falling to the shoulders in ringlets. The two back curls at the nape of the neck were called *crève-coeur* or heartbreakers. On the forehead were short curls in the form of a fringe. At the back, the hair was drawn into a knot or bun. Lace and ribbon bands and bows decorated the hair.

52 Corsets and panniers of the seventeenth and eighteenth centuries

Top left A seventeenth-century English corset. It was busked and stiffened with whalebone, and shaped into a deep point in front. The corset, when worn, was high under the armpits and over the breasts. The fastening was at the back by the lacing method. The front lacing was false.

Top right A corset of about 1660. It was the long, slim, close-fitting type with the basque-like short tabs which expanded over the hips. It was worn high under the arms. The corset was fastened both in the front and at the back.

Centre This corset, possibly of Dutch origin (1730–45), was close-fitting, finishing with short tabs. The fastening was both in the front and back. The shoulder pieces were also pulled in by lacing. The stomacher, which matched the corset, had a central slit which accomodated the stay-busk. In the lining at the top of the stomacher was a pocket.

Bottom This pannier structure (1730–50) was made from circular pieces of whalebone and enclosed within linen 'drums'. The slit over each hip was used as a pocket, the gown and the underskirt having matching slits. The separate panniers were sewn onto a tape waist band and attached to the body round the waist, with the panniers resting on each hip.

53 Officer in 'bucket boots', with a Lady, c. 1675

Tight lacing became the main feature of female costume in Europe at this time. The bodice was long-waisted, close-fitting and heavily boned, and sloped to a deep point in front. The low *décolletage* was cut more or less horizontally, surrounding the bosom and coming off the shoulders. It was edged with the lace of the chemise beneath. A bertha collar, sometimes called a 'falling whisk', completely enveloped the low neckline, and was fastened in the front by a jewelled brooch. Short tabs were often seen encircling the deep-pointed waistline and expanding over the hips. The bodice fastening was at the back. The short, straight ungathered sleeve, decorated with ribbon bows, finished just above the elbow and was joined to the sloping shoulders of the bodice. The frilled, full sleeve of the chemise fell from the outer sleeve to just below elbow level, and was often tied in the middle by a narrow ribbon band. The full open skirt was gathered at the waist in small pleats, then allowed to fall to the ground in loose folds. The open front revealed the petticoat of heavy silks and satins, and was sometimes profusely embroidered. The hair style worn had a parting round the front of the head with a fringe of flat curls arranged on the forehead; the side hair fell in ringlets to the shoulders. The back hair, as previously, was arranged in a bun and was decorated with pearls

and ribbon bows. The folding fan, often decorated with hand-painted pictures, was still very fashionable and popular.

With the passing of the petticoat breeches period, a great change in male attire followed. The doublet became a vest, and the jerkin and buff coat of military origin became the *justaucorps* or habit. The vest came to just below the waistline with the *justaucorps* falling to just above the knee. This French officer of the Gendarme à Cheval of *c.* 1675, wore the slightly waisted *justaucorps* with the skirts now considerably deeper than before. The *justaucorps* was now made of heavy cloth and was decorated from the collarless neckline to the hem with a close row of buttons and button-holes

English 'bucket boot'

in the brandenburg style. The pockets were placed low in the front in a vertical design, and were also decorated with buttons and button-holes. The sleeves were straight and close-fitting, ending in a deep turned-back cuff, concealed by large leather gauntlet gloves. The *justaucorps* was collarless, no doubt to accomodate the full wig that was worn. Around the neck was a cravat, or *jabot*, of lace or lawn which concealed the front opening of the shirt. From the right shoulder hung a broad leather baldrick which crossed the body, and from which hung the sword at the left hip. An embroidered sash ending in tassels was also worn around the waist. Full wide breeches fell to the knees. The large, high, military boots were worn. These were sometimes called 'Marlboroughs' or 'bucket boots', because of their very wide-flaring stiff knee-flaps. Broad, wide 'butterfly' spur leathers were also worn. Wigs were becoming very fashionable and this military gentleman wore a large French wig, known as the 'full bottomed' wig. The hair was shoulder length and hung down the back. Two front locks were plaited and tied with bows,

and fell over the shoulders in the front. The hat had a wide cocked brim in the front and back, with a moderately high crown. An ostrich plume fringe decorated the hat. Canes decorated with ribbon loops were often carried.

54   French Farmer and Milk-maid in country costume, c. 1678

The country fashions of *c.* 1678 followed as closely as possible the fashionable town fads and fancies. The French farmer wore the vest and *justaucorps*. The *justaucorps*, or coat, hung to just above the knees; the skirts had back and side slits. The neckline was round and without a collar. The coat was fastened from the neckline to the waist by a close row of buttons with braided button-holes. The pockets were set low and horizontally and had button and button-hole decoration. The sleeves were just below elbow length with deep turned-back cuffs from which emerged the full shirt sleeves. A neckcloth, a narrow linen scarf, was wound round the neck and was finished off with a loosely tied knot of ribbon loops. The breeches, or pantaloons, were wide and skirt-like; the large legs were pleated onto a waistband and fell to just below the knees. They were decorated at the sides with ribbon loops. The stockings were of the woollen variety. The shoes were square-toed, and the tongues over the instep hung down and were fastened with ribbon bows. The hairstyle of the countryman was natural but worn long, falling onto the back and shoulders. The moderately high crown of the hat was indented and attached to a fairly wide brim which was flat and straight all round. It was decorated with a ribbon hat band and a large bunch of ribbon loops.

The French country girl closely followed her female counterpart from the towns and cities regarding fashion, but with additions more practical for her needs. The bodice was long-waisted, close-fitting and boned, and came to a deep point in front. The *décolletage* was low cut, but was completely covered by a linen chemise with a neck frill. The full-length sleeves ended in turned-back cuffs. The skirt was gathered at the waist and hung in full folds to the ground, but contrary to the French law at that time, the young lady had hitched up her skirt

all round, *à la retroussée*, exposing the petticoat. The hair was parted in the centre and brushed back from the face. Covering the back of the head was a 'cornet', a coif style with long lappets or ear pieces which often fell behind the shoulders.

55 Children's fashions of the sixteenth to eighteenth centuries

Top left A small boy of *c.* 1564 wearing a jerkin over a doublet. The jerkin or jacket had a standing collar, and was fastened down the front from collar to waist. The skirts of the jacket were deep, almost hiding the trunk hose. At the shoulders were short, puffed wings with fairly close-fitting sleeves ending in wrist ruffs. The high neck was encircled with a small ruff, worn slightly open in front. The trunk hose sloped outwards from the waist and then turned into the thigh. Stocking hose were worn with round-toed, close-fitting leather shoes. A decorated tall-crowned hat with a narrow brim was worn.

Top right A young Spanish prince of the sixteenth century. Because he was unbreeched (i.e. had not reached the age of seven) he wore a dress with a stiff bodice. It had a deep point in front and a high neck encircled by a lace ruff. The winged sleeves were fairly close-fitting and ended with wrist ruffs; behind were hanging sleeves. The Spanish farthingale overskirt had an inverted V-shaped opening which revealed the underskirt.

Centre The young girl of *c.* 1632 wore the new style of dress with the basqued bodice tied at the waist with a ribbon cord. The bodice had sleeves which were ballooned and paned and caught mid-way at the elbows. They were called virago sleeves, and ended with wrist frills. The neckline was encircled with a laced falling band called a broad bertha. The skirt, which was gathered at the waist, fell to the ground in irregular folds. The hair was arranged with a forehead fringe and with the sides fluffed out. The back hair was brought up to a knot and was often decorated with feathers. Large feather fans were carried attached to the waist girdle by a ribbon cord.

Bottom left The young girl of *c.* 1740 wore a close-fitting bodice over a corset. The neckline was low and round, edged in lace. The waist was pointed in

front. The sleeves ended just above the elbows with a deep turned-back cuff from which emerged a hanging ruffle edged in lace. The skirt was worn over a dome-shaped hoop. On the head was worn a coif or round-eared cap. This curved round, framing the face, and was edged in lace.

Bottom right A young German boy *c.* 1560–80. He wore the close-fitting doublet with short tabbed skirts. The high neck was concealed by a small closed ruff. The doublet was fastened from neck to waist by buttons. The full sleeves, set under wings, ended at the wrists. The full, baggy pluder-hose, with the bulky waistline, followed the adult fashion. The shoes were slashed and paned. The boy wore the famous German 'barrett' hat with triangular pieces cut out and decorated with bunches of feathers.

56 Officer and his Lady, c. 1678

Before the middle of the 1670s, women's costumes were fashioned by tailors, but now they were made by dressmakers, milliners, etc., making fashion an extravagant and costly business. The bodice of the lady's costume was long and close-fitting. Being tightly corseted, the waist became smaller and the bust-line higher. The low *décolletage* was encircled with lace frills. The straight sleeves were elbow length and finished with lace ruffles. Long elbow-length, close-fitting gloves made of silk or fine leather were worn for all formal dress. The skirt was full and closely gathered in small pleats at the waist, then hung to the ground. An overskirt with a very long train was extremely fashionable. This was hitched up and bunched at the back over a pad, the forerunner of the bustle. The hem of the skirt was decorated with lace. The hair style consisted of a mass of short close curls all over the head. This coiffure was called a 'windblown bob' or by the peculiar name of 'hurluberlu'. The head-dress was the 'cornet'—a lawn cap which had a standing frill in front and long lappets falling behind the shoulders, or tied in front under the chin. The gauze veil was wired to stand proud over the forehead. Pinned on the front of the cap was a ribbon 'top knot' bow. Accessories, such as pomanders, were still carried, as was the folding fan.

The back view of the officer of *c.* 1678 shows the long body of the *justaucorps* with the skirts flaring out slightly from the low waistline. The coat was collarless and fastened down the front with buttons and fancy buttonholes. The back slit and the low horizontal pockets were also decorated in this way, but the side slits were usually unadorned. The sleeves were close-fitting to the elbows, then widened slightly, ending in a turned-back cuff. The cuff was often hidden by elegant, highly decorative, leather gauntlet gloves. On the right shoulder was worn a bunch of ribbon loops. Across the body from the right shoulder to the left hip was a long wide ornate baldrick which supported the sword. This was also decorated with ribbon loops, known as a

Gentleman's buckle shoe

'sword knot'. Around the waist was tied a silken sash with fringed ends. Wide breeches reaching to just below the knees were very popular. Square-toed shoes, which fastened with a buckle and strap, were worn; they had large tongues over the instep and often had coloured heels. Wigs with long ringlets laying over the shoulders were worn by all fashionable gentlemen. The wide brim of the felt hat was cocked high in front. It was edged with lace or braid, and trimmed with an ostrich feather fringe. At the back was a bunch of ribbon loops.

57 French Officer in 'bloomer' style with Lady, c. 1682

Although the ladies' costume of the bodice and skirt style continued to be worn, the gown began to be more popular from c. 1680. The tight-fitting, small-waisted bodice of the gown was joined to a full gathered skirt which was also trained. The décolletage formed round the back of the neck was either round or square, and was trimmed with a straight border which came over the shoulder to a deep V-shape at the waist. The gap was covered by a decorative stomacher which ended in a rounded point just below the waist. Often a fancy corset replaced the stomacher. The waist was encircled by a ribbon girdle with a spreading bow. The sleeves were short and straight, ending just above the elbow; they were turned and fastened just below the shoulder with a button and loop. From under these sleeves emerged the full chemise sleeves which finished at the elbows with lace ruffles. High elbow-length gloves fitted closely to the arms. The full skirt hung to the ground and the trained overskirt was hitched up behind and at the sides. The hair was taken back with curls over the temples and a centre parting. A bun or chignon was worn at the back. Over the head was a 'headkerchief' which fastened under the chin. Women's shoes tapered almost to a point, and like those of the males, they were fastened with buckles. A 'loo' mask was usually carried attached to the waist by a ribbon cord. Ivory handled walking canes and long handled parasols called 'umbrelloes' were carried.

The French officer wore the 'bloomer' style fashion. The coat was slightly waisted, with a short flared skirt falling to just below hip level. The collarless coat was fastened from neck to hem by buttons in fancy button-holes, as were the back slit and the low horizontal pockets. A knot of ribbon loops was worn on the right shoulder. The sleeves were close-fitting to just below elbow length, and had deep turned-back cuffs fastened and decorated with buttons. Around the neck was a linen cravat with a lace border. This was worn with a cravat string, which was a narrow band of ribbon tied in a bow under the chin. Across the body was the wide baldrick which supported the sword, and round the waist was a silk sash which was fringed at the ends. The 'bloomer' breeches were the closed type, but with wide legs gathered onto a band and fastened above the knee, finishing with a deep flounce. This flounce was turned up cuff-wise over the lower fullness of each leg, and sewn or attached at intervals to form large pleats. The breeches were fastened below the knee with ribbon ties and decorated with bunches of ribbon loops. The waist was also decorated with ribbon loops. The square-toed shoes were fastened over the long tongues with straps, large square buckles and limp bunches of ribbon loops. The shoes were usually black leather with red heels. The wigs of the soldiers were not as large as those for civilians and were called 'campaign' wigs. They were long, falling over the shoulders, and ended in two long corkscrew locks, or 'dildos', which could be tied back. The large, low-crowned hat had a very wide brim which was usually cocked on one side, or as personal taste required. The hat was decorated with coloured feather plumes. Gauntlet gloves were worn, often embroidered or trimmed with fur. Large fur muffs, a French fashion, were carried suspended on a ribbon round the neck.

'Bloomer' style breeches

58 Fashionable Gentleman and a peasant Girl, c. 1684

The French gentleman of fashion now wore his coat just above knee length, with a closer fit, and slight waisting more in evidence. The skirt fanned out from the pleats of the sewn side vents. The coat was collarless and fastened from neck to hem, but for the fashionable was always left open from just below the chest. The pockets could be worn high or low as the mode dictated. The sleeves were now longer, finishing nearer the wrist. The turned-back cuff was open at the back and had pointed corners known as 'hounds ears'. Down the front, around the skirt and around the cuffs, the coat was heavily decorated with buttons and braid. The neck was enclosed with a linen cravat and a large band of coloured ribbon tied into a wide spreading bow under the chin. The coat was worn without a waistcoat and revealed the full shirt beneath. The 'bloomer' leg breeches were still fashionable, but with less fullness. They were gathered onto a band just below the knee, with the fullness expanding slightly over the ribbon loop gartering. The flounce, *chausses à canons*, finished at the knee and was decorated with ribbon loops. The shoes tapered to a square-toe, and fastened over the high tongue with a strap and buckle. The wigs continued to be large, usually longer on the left side. The face was clean shaven, but sometimes a thin moustache was worn. The low-crowned hat, which had a very wide brim decorated with ribbon loops, was called a 'boater shape' hat. Large gauntlet gloves were fringed with lace and fur. Walking sticks were carried.

The French working-class woman's costume was without frills. The bodice was close-fitting and open to the waist in front but was filled in with a laced 'corset'. The waistline was at normal level. The skirt was gathered onto the bodice in close pleats and fell to ankle length. Full sleeves ended at the elbows and had turned or rolled-up cuffs without frills or ruffles. The neckline was cut low, and was round in the front and high at the back. Covering the neckline was a neckerchief of coarse linen. Also of coarse linen was the large apron in front which had a central pocket. The leather shoes tapered to a square toe and were fastened with a narrow ribbon tied in a spreading bow. The head was covered with a headkerchief wrapped around the hair. All the materials used for this costume were of a coarse quality.

59 Palace Guard Officer and Lady with a 'fontange', c. 1693

For the lady, the bodice was close-fitting and joined to a gathered and trained full skirt. The bordered neckline fitted high at the back of the neck in a round shape, and was brought over the shoulders to a V-shape at the waist, where it was fastened by a narrow buckled belt. The gap in front was filled-in with a stomacher which came to a point in the front and was decorated with trefoil scallops just below waist level. The straight sleeve ended just above the elbow with a turned-up cuff which was secured by a button and braid loop. The frilled ruffle of the chemise, often in multiple stages, dropped from the sleeve of the bodice. The trained skirt was taken back and hitched up, often over a bustle, *cul de Paris*. The exposed underskirt or petti-coat was trimmed at hip level with a reversed flounce, fringed with lace. The hem was embroidered with a lace edging. A military fashion which was taken up by the ladies was a Steinkirk cravat. This was a wide scarf of lawn wrapped around the neck, the ends being twisted together in front, then pinned to the left side of the bodice. Also pinned to the breast of the bodice was a *boutonnière*, a small bouquet of flowers. High, close-fitting elbow-length gloves were worn. The hair style was called the 'fontange' coiffure, or the 'tower'. The hair was arranged in curls at the front and wired up above the forehead, two peaks were formed with a centre parting, and, as its name implied, this hairdo was worn with the 'fontange' head-dress. This consisted of a close-fitting linen cap worn at the back of the head, with a structure of stiff linen frills, and two long linen streamers hanging down the back. A folding fan was still very fashionable. Patches, or 'mouches' —the popular name for black patches — were worn on the face as a mark of beauty.

The male dandy of the period wore the mixed fashions of the

day. The coat was close-fitting
down to the waist, the skirts
flaring out to mid-thigh. The
fastening was from the collarless
neckline to the hem with buttons and braid button-holes. The
coat was closed to chest level
only, then worn open to reveal the chemise shirt beneath.
The pockets were set very low,
about 10 cm from the hem-line,
and decorated with buttons and
braid. A tasselled handkerchief
was often hung from one of the
pockets. The side vents were
decorated with bunches of ribbon
loops as was the right shoulder.
The sleeves were tight-fitting,
ending near the wrist with a
turned-up cuff. From this cuff
emerged a deep ruffle, decorated
with ribbon bows. This extremely fashionable officer wore the
petticoat breeches style in lawn
and lace, lavishly trimmed with
ribbon loops round the waist, and
lace flounces hanging down either
side. The full breeches ended
just below the knees and were
tied with ribbon garters with
hanging loops. The shoes tapered
to a square toe, altering little
from the previous fashion. The
wig of long ringlets fell over the
shoulders, and was decorated
with ribbon bows. The large

Back view of 'fontange'

brimmed hat with the low crown
was cocked on one side and
decorated around the edge with
braid and ostrich feathers, and on
the left side with ribbon loops.
A tall cane bedecked with ribbon
bows and a sword were carried.

60 Gentleman of quality and a fashionable Lady, c. 1694

The silhouette of the female
changed very little during the
1690s. The close-fitting bodice
with the full, gathered and
trained skirt worn open in front
continued in fashion. Often the
stomacher was exchanged for an
embroidered corset. The sleeves
remained short to the elbow with
a turned-up cuff and deep ruffles
emerging below. The bustle
effect became very apparent with
the hitching back of the trained

overskirt. The underskirt or petticoat became very ornamental and decorative. Around the neck was worn a 'pallatine' or tippet of sable; this was a scarf of fur tied loosely around the neck with the two ends dangling down either side. A medium-sized muff of matching fur was carried. The hair was parted in the centre and wired up above the forehead forming two high peaks on either side, then fashioned onto the 'fontange' head-dress. The fontange was tall and narrow, with one tier built over another, reaching a considerable height. It was shaped like a half-closed fan tilting slightly forward. The two

long linen streamers were often pinned up to the crown.

With the passing of the full petticoat fashion, men's coats became slightly more waisted with flared skirts coming down to knee length. They fastened from the still collarless neckline to the hem with buttons, but were now left completely open. The pockets were higher, nearer the waist, and decorated with buttons. The sleeves were close-fitting, with very large, deep turned-back cuffs also ornamented with buttons. Around the neck was the fashionable Steinkirk cravat. The waistcoat, similar to the coat, was close-fitting and ended just above the knee. It fastened from the collarless neckline to the hem with buttons, but was usually open down to the chest, and was decorated with buttons and braid. Close-fitting, knee-length breeches, almost concealed by the coat, were fastened below the knee with either buttons or buckles. Shoes did not alter to any great extent. The wigs continued to be large and more artificial looking. The wide-brimmed hat edged with braid and decorated with feathers, was worn cocked to one side or in

Steinkirk neckwear

Gentleman's muff

whatever manner fashion decreed. Carrying a snuffbox became very popular. The fashionable dandy of the day wore a large muff suspended on a sash from around the waist.

61 Nobleman and his Son, c. 1695

The closing years of the seventeenth century brought no essential changes in fashionable male dress. The coats were close-fitting to the waist with flaring skirts in various lengths. The pleated side vents and the back slit still dominated the coat. The coat was usually collarless and fastened down the front with buttons. Usually all buttons, or those from the neck to the waist or from the chest to the hem, were left unfastened, according

to the fashionable whim of the time. The sleeves were close-fitting with large or medium size turned-back cuffs. Cravats were of linen with lace borders. The breeches were, in most cases, plain and close-fitting. They were fastened at the knee by buttons or buckles. Cloaks, if worn, were hung over both shoulders. The essential items of fashion were the large wigs of tight curls evenly arranged and framing the face. Shoes did not alter.

The boy was dressed in the same style and fashion as his elders. The only difference was that he wore his own hair; children never took up the fashionable adornment of wigs.

62 Late seventeenth- and early eighteenth-century shoe fashions

Top left Pointed-toed shoes embroidered in brocade with ribbon binding, c. 1730–50. A moderately high upper ending in a squared tongue fastened over the instep with a ribbon lace. The patten (shown below) which was worn over the shoe was made of leather, the sole being made in the same shape as the shoe. It was laced over with ribbon ties.

Top right A shoe from *c.* 1660–80 which was covered with silk braid and had an embroidered centre piece. The high uppers, finishing with a square tongue, fastened with strap and buckle. The high 'Louis' heel was popular.

Centre left A leather shoe, *c.* 1730–50, with an embroidered centre and a short, square tongue. It fastened with a jewelled buckle over the instep.

Centre right c. 1730. A lady's satin slipper with a matching heel bound with ribbon. It had an all-round deep frill of lace with a ribbon rosette over the instep.

Centre bottom left c. 1700. A mule of embroidered silk with a pointed toe and no heel. It was decorated with a lace frill and ribbon knot.

Bottom left A satin slipper or mule, *c.* 1660–88, with a thick solid heel. The slipper tapered to a square toe. Across the high instep was a pleated lace frill.

Bottom right This type of slipper was worn by both sexes. It was made in embroidered silk and had a tapering square toe with a very high tongue over the instep which was bound with ribbon.

63 Officer with snuffbox, and Lady, c. 1698

The French officer wore the fashion of the 1690s, with the close-fitting coat and the flaring skirts which ended just above the knees. The fastening was from the round collarless neck to the hem of the coat with a close row of buttons and braided button-holes. The pockets were horizontal and very low, only about 10 cm from the hem; they were also decorated with buttons and braid. The sleeves were close-fitting, ending in a turned-back cuff from which emerged the sleeve of the shirt with ribbon bows. The neck was covered by a cravat and a ribbon bow. Over the shoulder was a broad baldrick from which hung the sword with the ribbon loops or knots. Encircling the waist was a fringed silk sash. The breeches were full, ending just above the knees. Shoes remained fairly constant throughout this period. The long ringlet wig, which hung over the shoulders and back, was ornamented with ribbon bows. The wide-brimmed hat was feather trimmed and decorated with ribbon bows. An ornamented snuff container was carried.

The lady's gown was the height of fashion at this time. The bodice, open in front to the waist, was filled in either by a stomacher or an embroidered 'corset'. The bodice came up to the neck at the back and was edged in folds of muslin. The 'fill-in' was of soft lawn and it completely covered the *décolletage*. The gathered, trained skirt was joined to the bodice and hitched up towards the bustle-like back. The exposed petticoat was heavily embroidered around the hips and at the hem with heavy ruffles or 'furbelows'. The fashionable hair coiffure was worn with the very popular *bonnet à la Fontanges*. Moderately sized muffs were carried.

64 French General with Lady in riding habit, c. 1704

The clothes of the fashionable male kept to a more constant design, and varied only in cut. Materials now played a more essential part for both formal and informal dress. The French officer wore the close-fitting coat reaching just below the knees. The skirt vents remained, as in the past decades, the open slit at the back and two pleated side vents reaching to hip level. The neck of the coat was low and collarless. The coat was fastened from neck to hem by dome-shaped, medium-sized buttons surrounded by heavy ornamentation or 'frogging'. These buttons, however, were purely decorative as the coat was left completely open. The sleeves were close-fitting and ended with deep, round turned-back cuffs, also buttoned and ornamented. The frilled shirt sleeve cuffs emerged from below the coat sleeve cuff. The waistcoat was embroidered and was open to just below the chest to reveal the Steinkirk neckwear. The knee breeches were fastened just below the knee with a kneeband. The stockings were made of silk and embroidered. The shoes tapered to a square toe, with the uppers covering the foot and finishing in long square tongues which drooped over the instep. A wide silk sash encircled the waist. The full-bottomed French wig remained in fashion with a mass of curls framing the face, then falling down the back and over the shoulders. The cocked hat, or tricorne, was worn. It was decorated round the edge with gold braid and an ostrich feather plume fringe. A cane and sword were carried.

The ladies' riding attire was similar to that of men and had a back slit and two pleated side vents in the jacket. The jacket was close-fitting to the waist, then the skirts flared out to just below knee level. It fastened from the round collarless neck to the hem with buttons. The pockets were set low, near the hem. The sleeves were close-fitting and ended with a turned-back cuff, from which emerged the full sleeve of the chemise. Around the neck was the Steinkirk neckwear. Under the jacket was a waistcoat similar to those worn by the male. The petticoat was long, full, and often trained. The wig was a copy of the elaborate full-bottomed wig which rose up in two points on each side of a central parting. A tricorne hat and short riding stick were carried.

Night cap

65 Gentleman in morning gown, c. 1712

Morning gowns of Oriental and Asian design were worn by men as négligées. The morning gown was not unlike the dressing gown worn by men to-day. It was a loose gown which fell to just below the knee, and had a roll collar and a wrap-over front. The full sleeves were turned or rolled back from the wrists, with the frilled sleeves of the shirt emerging below. The gown often tied at the waist with a sash. It came in a variety of materials such as damask, brocade, satin, chintz and silk. Although in most cases the gown was worn with a nightcap, it was not uncommon for a gentleman to remove his coat and vest and then don his morning gown for ease. The large full-bottom wig was still popular and was divided into three parts; one down the back and the other two down either shoulder. Powder was used to clean the wigs, and being light brown or whitish grey in colour, tended to give a greying effect. Perfume was also used on wigs. To accommodate these hot and cumbersome wig styles, the hair was either cut very short or completely shaven off.

66 Officer and his Lady, c. 1720

This was a period when fashion looked backwards for the female styles. The lady is wearing a separate bodice and skirt. The bodice of the jacket, doublet or *casaquin* was close-fitting to the waist where the skirt was basqued and flared out over the petticoat. The *décolletage* was low in front; it was round in shape and edged with narrow lace. The bodice fastened down the front to the waist by hooks and eyes, concealed by a fly closure. The sleeves were close-fitting and ended just below the elbow; the frilled cuff of the chemise emerged below. The petticoat was untrimmed and worn over dome-shaped hoops. This costume was worn for the 'undress' fashion. The hair style was simple, close to the head and off the forehead.

The military officer is dressed in a low-necked collarless coat which buttoned from neck to hem but was always worn open. The sleeves were close-fitting and ended with a deep turned-back cuff, from which the frilled cuff of the shirt sleeve emerged. The waistcoat, decorated similarly to the coat, was worn open at the chest to reveal the cravat. The cravat consisted of a strip of lawn wound round the neck and then loosely tied under the chin; the two ends left dangling were edged with lace. A silken sash encircled the waistcoat. Close-fitting knee breeches were enclosed under heavy jack-boots which reached above the knees with slightly flaring 'bucket tops'. The boots were square-toed and worn with spur leathers and metal spurs with star rowels. The campaign wig was worn; this framed the face from a central parting and fell on to both shoulders. Plain leather gauntlet gloves were carried. The three cornered hat with the low crown was worn. The brim was decorated with braid.

67 Early eighteenth-century corset fashions

Top An underbodice of *c.* 1720. This was a padded bodice with a deep, rounded skirt. It was never exposed, and was most probably worn for warmth under the dress.

Bottom left This was a corset of *c*. 1715. It was close-fitting and deeply pointed in the front, with flaring pickadils which expanded over the hips. The corset, made of brocade, was reinforced with whalebone stiffeners, and rose high under the armpits and over the bosom. It was fastened at the back with lacing and the shoulder straps were decorated with ribbon bows.

Bottom right The corset style of *c*. 1725 fitted close to the waist and came to a deep round point in the front. At waist level were pickadils which expanded out over the hips. The corsage of the corset was high at the back in a rounded shape, but low in the front where it encircled the bosom, rising high under the armpits, and to a point at the centre front. From this point down to the waist it was fastened with lacing. The corset was stiffened with whalebone stays. It was made from a damask material.

68 Lady in riding habit wearing a Steinkirk cravat, c. 1720

As horse riding was an essential part of life, and also a fashionable sport, women who followed this pursuit wore the more practical styles of their day. The female riding habit, apart from the petticoat, was therefore a copy of the male fashion. The coat followed the mode of the collarless coat for men. It had a back slit and two pleated side vents which gave the stand-out effect. The coat had fastenings from neck to hem, but was left open revealing the close-fitting waistcoat, which was fastened at the waist only. The fastening of both the coat and the waistcoat followed the male fashion of being buttoned left over right. The top opening showed the popular neckwear, namely the Steinkirk cravat. The opening from the waist down showed the deep inverted flounce of the petticoat at about midthigh level. The petticoat was full and fell to about ankle depth. The hem was surrounded by a deep lace border. The hair was covered by a full wig, again following the male fashion. This framed the face and fell down the back and on either side. The male tricorne, or three cornered hat, was worn or carried. A tasselled riding crop was carried, and short gauntlet gloves of the riding type were worn.

69 Fashionable Gentlemen of quality, c. 1725

The male costumes still retained the *justaucorps* vest and breeches of the previous era, but with modifications, giving them an ease and elegance.

The two gentlemen are wearing similar outfits. The coat was close-fitting and waisted with the fully flared skirt reaching to just below the knees; the length depending on the fashionable whim of the time. The back centre slit and the two side slits, which were the continuation of the side seams, continued to be worn. The side slits were pleated with five or six pleats, sewn down at the top of the slit just beneath a hip button. The slits, however, were never completely closed, to allow the sword, when worn, to come through. The coat was without a collar and was cut rather low in front. The leading edge of the coat fell in a straight line down the front. It fastened with buttons and button-holes from the neck to waist level; the buttons below were purely decorative. The pockets were horizontal and covered with oblong flaps, usually triple scalloped. The sleeves were close-fitting with deep cuffs ending well above the wrist. This allowed the full shirt sleeve with wrist ruffle to appear below. The gentleman standing wore the round cuff; the gentleman sitting wore the 'boot' cuff. The vest, or waistcoat, closely resembled the coat. It was close-fitting to the waist and had flaring skirts stiffened with buckram. The vest was now worn well above the knees, the back often being made of an inferior material to that of the front. The fastening was with buttons and button-holes from neck to hem. It fastened by one or two buttons at the neck and was then open to the waist, revealing the ruffles at the neck. It was again fastened at the

Cuff detail

waist, by one or two buttons, and then unfastened to the hem; these lower buttons were usually ornamental. The pocket of the vest was similar to the coat pocket. The breeches were gathered onto a waist band with the leg narrowing downwards, finishing just below the knee in a kneeband over the stocking. A short slit up the outer seam of the breeches was closed by three small buttons. The shoes had blocked square toes with square high heels. The uppers of the shoes finished in square tongues which were high in front of the ankle. The sides were closed and the fastening was by straps and buckles over the instep.

The standing gentleman wore a costume of velvet and a campaign wig. The wig was bushy, parted in the middle, with ridges of waved hair on either side of the parting. It was arranged to fall down the back where it was tied in a knot.

The sitting gentleman wore a suit of clothes of damask satin. The wig was the undress type called a 'caxon' wig. This was a tie wig of pale straw or off-white colour. The hair was drawn back with the curls bunched together to form a queue, and tied with a black ribbon bow at the nape of the neck.

70 Officer in armoured breastplate with Lady, c. 1727

The bodice of the female gown changed very little except in small details, such as the low *décolletage* and short sleeves. Both closed and open gowns were worn. The lady depicted wore the closed robe with a bodice that had short robings and a stomacher front, similar to that worn with the open gown, but with a front fall fastening to the petticoat. The bodice was very close-fitting with a low, round neckline. A handkerchief or modesty piece and tucker was always worn to cover the low *décolletage*. The back of the bodice was also close-fitting and joined the skirt with double box pleats or *corsage en fourreau*. The skirt was made with a short fall at the front pleated onto a waistband. This gown was worn with dome-shaped hoops, often called 'pocket hoops', which were for day use only. The sleeves finished at the elbows with frilled cuffs appearing below. Long elbow-length gloves fitted close to the arms. The undress mop cap was worn with the border encircling the face and the side pieces dangling down either side like lappets.

The military gentleman wore the fashionable coat, vest and breeches of the day. Over this he wore the sign of his profession—the last vestige of a by-gone age—armour. The chest and back were covered with the *cuirass* and *epaulières* which were the guards for the shoulders; the upper arms were covered with *brassarts*. Over the front of the thighs were two small shield-shaped pieces secured by straps and buckles, which allowed free movement of the limbs. These were called *garde-faude*, *tuille* or tassets. All the armour was lined and had a bordered edge formed by the lining. A baldrick and waist

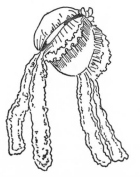

Cap with lappets

sash were worenn, doting the high rank of the officer. High 'bucket top' boots were worn with spur leathers and spurs. The campaign wig, tied at the back with a ribbon bow, was surmounted by the cocked hat of the military style, called a 'kevenhuller hat'. The brim was bound in open-work lace and edged with a feather fringe. A 'cockade', in place of the normal button and loop, was favoured by some military men.

71 Lady wearing a mantua, and Gentleman in redingote, c. 1729

The lady shows the back view of the 'mantua' style gown. This was basically an open robe, but worn with a petticoat. The close-fitting, long-waisted bodice was unboned and shaped to the underlying corset. The corset, replacing the stomacher, could have been embroidered or plain in front. The bodice was edged with smooth flat revers which overlapped and were known as 'robings'. They formed a straight line across the back of the neck and then continued over the shoulders down to waist level in the front. The close-fitting sleeves ended just

Redingote collar detail

below the elbow with turned-up cuffs; the chemise sleeve and ruffle edged in lace appeared below. The gathered petticoat was pleated onto a waistband and secured behind, falling in loose folds to the ground. It was quite plain and without flounces. The petticoat was worn over a structure called the 'capula' or 'bell hoop' made of distended hoops of whalebone or cane. The round-eared cap was worn, and being bonnet-shaped, framed the face with the frilled front border. At the back, the cap was made to fit by pulling a draw-string. Side lappets were attached to the lower edge of the cap and hung down either in front or behind.

The man wore the outdoor garment or greatcoat. This particular style was known as the redingote and was of English origin but became very popular in France. It was worn in inclement weather and for riding. The heavy cloth redingote was full but was pulled in at the waist with the assistance of a belt; the pleated flaring skirt reaching below the knees. The fastening was double-breasted with buttons and large button-holes. The neckline was encircled by two deep flat collars; the top collar fastened up over the mouth and up to the ears. The straight sleeves had very deep turned-back cuffs to elbow depth, where they were fastened by buttons. The full shirt sleeve cuff appeared below. The square-toed shoes had a long, high tongue which rose in front of the ankle. The shoes were buckled over the instep. The tricorne hat was worn over a powdered bag-wig, which had a large bow at the back.

72–73 Ladies in the voluminous 'robe battante', c. 1729

The *sacque* or sack dress originated in France in the 1720s, and was the principal style of the French regency. When this style first came to England it was worn as a négligée for indoor use only, but later it became so popular that it was worn for all occasions. For these voluminous skirts heavy damasks and brocades were replaced by cottons and silks. This type of gown had such names as 'robe battante', or 'Watteau flying gown' after the paintings by Jean Antoine Watteau. Sometimes the materials were quilted with woollen stuff for extra warmth.

The gown on the left had a shaped bodice over a corset. The bodice was open with the robings crossing the shoulders at the back and coming down either side to the waist. The space in the opening of the bodice was filled in with a plain stomacher pinned to the tabs and joined under the robings. Across the top of the stomacher was a lace tucker. The sleeves were close-fitting, ending in a large cuff, from which emerged the chemise sleeve ruffle. On the bodice were pinned bosom flowers, either real or artificial. The skirt was joined to the bodice and closed all round, under this was a full closed petticoat. The shape of the gown was governed by the structure of the hoop, a popular one being the fan hoop.

The Dutch coiffure was the fashion of the period, and was popular for some years. Artificial flowers were also worn in the hair.

The gown on the right was very large and rather shapeless, falling from the low rounded neckline to the hem in a tent-like appearance. There were no robings, and a tucker was worn. The front had an edge to edge fastening by hooks and eyes. The bodice back was closer fitting and was attached to the skirt *corsage en fourreau*, which were box pleats doubled to give further fullness at the back, then falling in a flowing manner. The pyramidal fan-shape hoop was worn under the voluminous sack skirt and petticoat which fell to the ground forming a large circle. The sleeves finished at elbow length with deep cuffs and ruffles appearing below. Elegant, close-fitting gloves of elbow length were worn. Artificial flowers were used as hair decoration and on the corsage.

74 Lady and Gentleman in Highland costume, c. 1745

There seems to be no absolutely authentic surviving portrait

Early type of sporran

showing how a Highland lady looked when dressed in her fashionable finery. This plate depicts the wrap-over gown without hoops, but with the full ruffle sleeves and a modesty piece. The lady is seen wearing the tartan screen or plaid, often worn by Scottish ladies to show their Jacobite sympathies. It was very popular in Scotland during the eighteenth century. The hair was fashioned in the style of the Dutch coiffure.

The gentleman is wearing the complete Highland costume of coat, trews and plaid. Trews were mainly worn by the chiefs of clans as they preferred to ride on horseback, as opposed to clansmen who wore kilts and walked. The jacket buttoned down the front, was hip-length and had a turn-over flat collar. Around the neck was worn a white stock. The trews were close-fitting breeches with the kneebands buckled below the knees over the stockings. From the right shoulder was a broad leather crossbelt which supported a claymore type sword on the left side. Encircling the waist was a black leather belt which secured the dirk dagger in front. Over the left shoulder was slung the plaid, or wrap-around cape. The fashionable bag-wig was worn. The tartan shown on this plate is the black and red of the Rob Roy tartan.

In 1747 the English Government passed the 'Dress Act' which made it illegal 'to wear or put on the clothes commonly known as Highland clothes, which is plaid, philabeg or little kilt, trowse, shoulder belt or any part whatsoever which belongs to the Highland garb; no tartan or party-coloured plaid or stuff shall be used for great coats or for upper coats'. To disobey this Act meant six months imprisonment for the first offence and transportation to the colonies for seven years for the second.

75 Lady in a quilted petticoat, c. 1745

This dress of silk damask was in the open robe style, and was the most popular style of the period. The costume consisted of a bodice joined to a skirt which was open in the front to show the petticoat. Although its name implies an undergarment, it was in fact part of the costume and never hidden from view. The close-fitting bodice ended slightly below the normal waistline, and was lightly boned. It was open in front, with the edges bordered with short robings from around the neck over the shoulders to the waistline, and down either side. The opening of the bodice was filled in with a decorative stomacher, heavily embroidered with ribbon and lace. The stomacher was usually attached under the robings by pinning. The costume was worn over an oblong hoop which was flattened both front and back. The sleeves, which ended just above the elbow, were straight and close-fitting with small winged cuffs; the chemise sleeve ruffles emerged below. The petticoat was pleated onto a waistband and tied behind, it then fell in loose irregular folds to the ground. This particular petticoat was quilted to give both fullness and warmth. Long elbow-length gloves were worn. Over the head was a pinner, a lace bordered cap worn on the crown of the head. The lappets were turned up and pinned to the crown with a brooch or a jewel hat ornament.

76 Early eighteenth-century fashions

Top left A sack dress made in a stiff silk with broad vertical strips. The bodice was shaped to the figure. The sleeves ended at the elbow and had narrow turned-back winged cuffs, with ruffles appearing below. The sack-back was made of double box pleats on either side of the centre back seam, sewn down to shoulder level, then allowed to fall down the back. The petticoat was suspended on fan type hoops. A small white cap was worn.

Top right The back view of the gentleman's fashion of the period. The knee-length coat had a small stand collar and open cuffs. The breeches finished at the knees. The pigeon-winged toupee, which had one or two horizontal roll curls above the ears, was worn with a bag-wig. Over this was worn a tricorne.

Centre A frame, sometimes articulated, to carry the hooped petticoats. Pockets were tied round the waist and under the hoop structure, the petticoat having slits on either side.

Bottom left The milkmaid fashion with the close-fitting bodice and stomacher. This was the open robe style. The sleeves were close-fitting with flounces falling low behind. The elaborately arranged overskirt was pinned on either side of the panniers. The petticoat was gathered at the waist and fell in folds to the ground.

Bottom right A gentleman with the coat and vest, both fastening from neck to hem, but both unfastened in the fashionable way. He wore the full-bottomed wig which after 1750 went out of fashion.

77 Fashionable Lady with embroidered robings, c. 1750

This was a typical fashion of the 1740–50s. The bodice had a widespread *décolletage* with robings laying over the edge of the shoulders. The plain stomacher was also wide. The robings

crossed the back and came down either side to finish at the waist. Around the edge of the robings and across the top of the stomacher was a narrow lace frill or tucker. The sleeves were full to the elbows, then finished with three horizontal pleats, usually stitched down. From under the sleeves appeared the full sleeves of the chemise with deep double ruffles. High elbow-length gloves enclosed the lower arms. The skirt was worn over a dome-shaped hoop. The Dutch coiffure was worn, which consisted of the front hair waved back from the forehead, and the ears just visible below the hair at the temple. At the back there were a few ringlets at the nape of the neck; these were entwined with a ribbon knot. Over this hair style was a pinner which rested on the crown of the head; the lappets were drawn up to the crown and pinned up.

78 Madame de Pompadour, c. 1755

The sack gown, called by the French *robe à la française*, was worn at this period as an open robe, both for formal and informal use. The close-fitting bodice was open. The robings went round

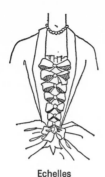

Echelles

the back of the neck, over the shoulders, and then carried on down to the hem of the gown. The gap in the open bodice was filled by a stomacher with a series of ribbon bows, decreasing in size down to the waist. These were known as *échelles*, and were very fashionable and popular throughout the eighteenth century. The stomacher was attached by pins to the tabs which were fastened under the robings. The sleeves ended just above the elbows and were close-fitting to the arms. They were decorated with a spreading ribbon knot at the elbow. Appearing below the sleeves were deep treble ruffles of lace which ended at about mid-arm. The overskirt and the petticoat adapted themselves to the type and shape of hoop worn. This gown had the dome shape. The

supporting petticoat was usually made of buckram, the required shape being formed by distended hoops of whalebone or cane. It was attached around the waist by a draw-string. The petticoat was flounced and furbelowed. A lace ruff was worn round the neck. The hair was brushed back from the forehead and temples, the hair at the back being brushed up and formed into a small bun on the crown of the head. Pearls and ribbon often decorated the bun. Fresh flowers were often worn pinned to the bodice. Folding fans retained their popularity.

79 Guards Officer with Lady, c. 1758

The lady wears the open robe gown with a trained overskirt, to which was joined the bodice. The robings crossed the outer edge of the shoulders and carried on down to the hem of the overskirt. The broad stomacher was trimmed with *échelles*, or bows, decreasing in size down to the waist. The stomacher was usually fastened to the robings by tabs which projected for this reason. The sleeves, which fitted well into the

227

back of the bodice, were tight-fitting, ended at the elbows and were decorated with large ribbon knots. Ruffles trimmed with frills of lace extended from the sleeves. Around the wide square-necked *décolletage* and around the shoulders was crossed a chiffon 'handkerchief' which was fastened at the bosom. The petticoat was closely pleated into a waistband and tied at each side, falling into loose folds to the ground. It was trimmed with inverted flounces at about knee level. The popular elbow-length gloves were worn. The simple styled 'milkmaid' hat of natural straw was worn squarely on the head over the low insignificant coiffure. The hair was combed straight back, and twisted into a bun on the top of the head.

The officer wears the gala or dress uniform of the 1st Battalion of the Guards Infantry Regiment of the Prussian army of that period. This uniform was very much admired and immediately copied by other administrations. The chief characteristic was the evenly spaced rows of large loops and buttons which decorated the front and cuffs of the coat. The white gaiters were worn for summer uniform only. The hat was ornamented with silver lace and white ostrich plumage around the top.

80 Lady in 'bergère' hat with Gentleman Officer, c. 1760

The gown worn by the lady was in the trained sack-back style made in a delicately patterned brocade. The wide *décolletage*, square in shape, was covered by a crossed 'handkerchief' of chiffon which draped across the bosom and fastened in front with a breast-knot bow. The short, tight sleeves fitted well into the back of the bodice, and finished just above the elbow with deep treble ruffles which reached almost to the wrist. Elbow-length gloves of thread, muslin, cotton or kid were worn, and came in a variety

Corset and stomacher

of colours. High-heeled shoes were worn and had such names as 'French' or 'Pompadour'. The 'bergère' or 'milkmaid' straw hat was very popular at this time. It was fairly simple in style, being round with a low crown and a wide brim which could be turned up either at the front or the back. Ribbon strings on either side were drawn back and tied in a bow on the nape of the neck. The hat was worn over a close-fitting undercap, usually made in white muslin, into which the hair was drawn back.

The gentleman officer wore the very fashionable loose-fitting, collarless coat known as the *justaucorps*. The skirts extended slightly outwards because of stiffening with buckram or whalebone. The coat fastened from the neck to the hem with buttons. The centre back vent also fastened by buttons from the hem to the waist. The sleeves were straight with deep cuffs that were closed all round and ornamented with buttons and button-holes. Just below waist level were low-set pockets with deep flaps. The frilled shirt sleeves extended from the coat cuffs. A sleeveless waistcoat was worn; it was single breasted, hip length, and had flapped pockets at waist level. The closer fitting breeches which fastened at the knees were becoming more popular and long woollen stockings were worn under the knee-high riding boots which were fitted with steel spurs. The military black stock was worn forming a high neckband; it was buckled behind, leaving the ruffled shirt front uncovered and able to protrude in front. For military gentlemen the 'pig tail' wig was often worn. The queue was long and spirally bound with black ribbon, and usually tied with black bows above and below. The bows above and below. The three cornered hat was the accepted head wear. This, for the military, was broad brimmed, high cocked, and trimmed with a cockade which was fastened down with a button and loop. The brim was edged with gold lace. Around the waist was a broad sash or baldrick, under which was a sword belt supporting a military sword.

SOURCES OF ILLUSTRATIONS

41. *After* Wenceslaus Hollar and Daniel Mytens
42. *After* Wenceslaus Hollar and contemporary Continental Sources
43. *After* Van Dyck
44. *After* Wenceslaus Hollar
45. *After* Gerard ter Borch and Wenceslaus Hollar
46. *After* Original Specimens
47. *After* J. C. Meyern and Wenceslaus Hollar
48. *After* Diego de Silver Velázquez
49. *After* A. Van Tempel
50. *After* Gerard ter Borch
51. *After* Netscher
52. *After* various sources
53. *After* I. D. Saint–Jean and Gerard ter Borch
54. *After* Bonnart and I. D. de Saint–Jean
55. *After* various sources
56. *After* I. D. de Saint–Jean
57. *After* I. D. de Saint–Jean and contemporary Continental Sources
58. *After* Hyacinthe Rigaud and I. D. de Saint–Jean
59. *After* I. D. de Saint–Jean and contemporary Continental Sources
60. *After* Trouvain and I. D. de Saint–Jean

61. *After* Largillière and an Unknown Artist
62. *After* Eunice Wilson
63. *After* Bonnard and Contemporary Continental Sources
64. *After* Zur Geschichte der Kostüme and an Unknown Artist
65. *After* Jodokus Verbeek
66. *After* contemporary Continental Sources and Temple Newsom House, Leeds
67. *After* original specimens
68. *After* Godfrey Kneller
69. *After* Richard Waitt and contemporary Continental Sources
70. *After* William Hogarth and contemporary Continental Sources
71. *After* Hèrriset
72-73. *After* Nicolas Lancrete and Hèrriset
74. *After* Alan Ramsay
75. *After* an original specimen at The Gallery of the English Costume, Manchester
76. *After* various sources
77. *After* William Hogarth
78. *After* François Boucher
79. *After* Arthur Devis and Adolph Menzel
80. *After* Adolph Menzel and Henry Pickering

GLOSSARY

Aiglets	Metal tags used to join sleeves and the hose to doublet
Aigrettes	A standing plume of feathers worn on the head
Bagwig	The queue of the wig being placed in a black silk bag at the nape of the neck
Baldrick	A wide sash of silk or leather, worn over the right shoulder, supporting a sword
Band strings	Usually tasselled ties for fastening the ruffs in front
Basque	A very short overskirt sewn on to the bodice
Bents	Strips of bone or wood to distend farthingales
Bertha	A deep collar of lace or silk which encircled the neck and shoulders
Bombast	Padding and stuffing to distend garments, made from cotton, wool, horsehair, etc.
Bongrace	An oblong stiffened head piece which projected over the forehead and hung down the back of the head to the shoulders
Brandenburgs	Ornamental fastenings of braided loops and buttons
Buff coat	A sleeveless military coat made of ox hide, later worn by fashionable civilians
Bum roll	A padded roll used for distending the skirt at the hips
Campaign wigs	Military type wigs worn with short side locks and a short queue behind
Canions	Extensions from the trunk hose to the knees, being close thigh fitting
Cartwheel ruff	A large stiffly starched collar which encircled the neck, about a quarter of a metre wide
Castellated	Decorative slashings of the edges of garments, into square cut edges
Caul	A cap of a network made in silk or gold thread, often lined with silk
Cavalier hat	Type of hat worn by the Royalists of England
Caxon wig	(or tie wig) Worn for undress and usually white in colour
Chaperone	A headdress which consisted of a hood and small shoulder cape in one
Chemise	An undergarment of linen worn by both male and female
Cloak bag breeches	Baggy and oval shaped breeches fitted just above the knee

Cod-piece	Of Spanish origin, a small bag formed at the fork of men's hose
Coif	A bonnet type close fitting cap
Copotain hat	A hat with a high conical crown with a narrow brim
Cornet hat	Made of lace and worn in various styles, as a day cap
Décolletage	The low neckline of a lady's dress
Doublet	A bombast jacket usually close fitting and waisted
Echelles	A stomacher which was trimmed down the front with ribbon bows
Falling band collar	A collar which lay on the shoulders without a support
Farthingale or verdingale	A structure in various shapes expanding the skirt by means of hoops from bone, wood etc.
Fontange	A linen cap with tall erections of lace or linen frills supported by a wire frame
French hood	Small bonnet worn at the back of the head the front border curving round the ears
Frogging	Decorative loop fastenings for a coat
Full-bottomed wig	Large wig with a centre parting with curls framing the face, shoulder length
Golillia	Spanish for the standing collar round the back of the head
Guards	Borders either plain or decorated to conceal the seams
Hanger type sword	Worn from a waist belt and frog, usually worn under the coat
Justaucorps	The French name for a man's close-fitting coat worn over a waistcoat
Lappet	Lace or linen pieces attached to a cap, usually hanging down on either side of the face
Mantua gown	A loose unboned bodice gown worn with an open front revealing a petticoat, fitted with a long train
Medici collar	A standing collar round the back of the neck and made from net or lace
Négligée	A term used by both male and female for informal dress
Nether stocks	The lower stocking portion of the hose
Pallatine	A shoulder wrap for ladies
Panes	Produced either by slashing or strips of ribbon set close together
Pannier	The French name for the side hoops
Partlet	A type of chemisette or 'fill in' for a low decolletage
Pattens	Overshoe footwear made of wood and raised by means of an iron stand
Peascod belly	Formed by padding the front of the doublet and overhanging the girdle

Pickadils	A tabbed or scalloped order used on doublet skirts and as supports for the ruff
Pinner	The lappets of a cap being pinned up. Later becoming just a plain cap with a frill
Pluderhose	German name for the wide baggy trunk-hose
Points	Ties used to attach the male trunk-hose to the doublet and the female sleeves and gowns
Pommander	A suspended receptacle which contained perfume
Queue	The hanging tail of a wig
Rhinegrave	Known also as 'petticoat breeches' worn in the style of a divided skirt decorated with ribbon bows
Ribbon knots	Clusters of various coloured ribbon loops, worn by both sexes
Ribbon loops	Usually worn in clusters and decorated both male and female costumes
Robings	Flat trimmings decorating a gown round the neck and the front of the bodice
Sack gown	A loose gown consisting of box pleats sewn into the back, from the neck line to the shoulder
Slashings	A symmetrical arrangement of slits in various lengths, the lining being pulled through as decoration
Slop hose	Wide breeches effected by sailors but civilian fashion in the 16th and 17th centuries
Steinkirk	a long cravat, loosely knotted, the ends threaded through a button hole or pinned to one side. Worn by both sexes
Sweet gloves	Scented Spanish leather gloves
Taffeta pipkin	A small hat with a flat crown drawn into a narrow brim
Tippet	A short shoulder cape originally a medieval liripipium
Trunk hose	The extended portion of male leg-wear from the waist, joining the stockings at the fork
Trunk sleeves	Often called 'cannon sleeves', were wide at the top becoming close-fitting to the wrist
Underpropper	A wire structure fixed at the back of the neck to support a large ruff
Vandyke beard	A fashion worn at the time and painted by the artist Van Dyke
Venetian breeches	Wide pear-shaped padded hose which reached and fastened just below the knee
Wings	Projections over the shoulder seams of the doublets or bodices.